TOP COACH

BADMINTON

BADMINTON

DEREK TALBOT

Macdonald
Queen Anne Press

A Queen Anne Press BOOK

First published in Great Britain in 1989 by
Queen Anne Press, a division of
Macdonald & Co (Publishers) Ltd
66 - 73 Shoe Lane,
Holborn, London EC4P 4AB
A member of Maxwell Pergamon Publishing Corporation plc

This book was designed and produced by
Sackville Design Group Ltd
Hales Barn, Stradbroke, Suffolk IP21 5JG

Editor: Philippa Algeo
Designers; Rolando Ugolini, Helen Whitworth
Illustrations: Rolando Ugolini

British Library Cataloguing in Publication Data
    Talbot, Derek
    Top Coach Badminton
    1. Badminton — Manuals
    I. Title
    796.34'5
    ISBN 0-356-17913-3

Typeset by BPCC Printec Ltd, Norfolk, England
Reproduction by BPCC Bury Studio, Bury St Edmunds, Suffolk, England

Printed and bound in Spain by Graficas Reunidas S.A., Madrid

Contents

Foreword

This book is unique in that it draws together an élite group of badminton experts to cover all aspects of the game. It is true that no one person can provide a complete approach to a sport, so I have selected people who are of world repute in their specialist departments of the game to provide for the reader the very best opinion. Many of these co-authors do not have the time to write a complete book and their opinions and experience would otherwise be lost forever.

The contents of this book are aimed principally at the ambitious club player but much of the information is relevant to players of all standards from beginner to international level. I cannot stress enough the importance of learning to play correctly as old habits die hard and many are impossible to remove. Indeed quite often when a player progresses to international level many faults picked up in their formative years present tremendous barriers to further progress. Coaches and players alike should appreciate that good technique is essential and hopefully this book will enable particularly the grass roots player to learn the game correctly. Remember from little acorns oak trees grow and even the world champion started as a beginner.

Coaches who are responsible for teaching in schools, colleges and starter clubs will hopefully benefit from the contents of this book. The efforts of coaches are so important to the growth and general welfare of badminton. We are all part of a sport which is about to grow tremendously on a world-wide basis over the next few years. In the UK alone more than four million people play badminton, a total which is greater than the combined players of tennis and squash. As a new member of the Olympic movement badminton's development throughout more than 90 countries will be extensive and its suitability to such a status is all the more deserved for it is enjoyed almost equally by men and women alike.

I am sure after reading this book you will appreciate that while one can enjoy playing badminton as part of a healthy lifestyle the demands of world-class play are intense. Indeed badminton players not only need to be complete athletes but they also need a sharp brain to be good. Such variation of enjoyment makes our sport truly unique and I hope this collection of experts' advice will encourage some readers to take up the sport, others to improve the standard of their play, but overall for everyone to enjoy this wonderful game, badminton.

Derek Talbot

Derek Talbot

Far right: Derek Talbot was undoubtedly one of the top international players of the seventies. His career now centres around commenting on badminton for television, and his sports equipment business.

Chapter 1 Equipment and Facilities

Below: This simple test reveals the balance point of a racket — 30cm/12" from the base. In addition, the strings should be of even and high tension.

The development of equipment for badminton has come a long way since the origin of the game at the Duke of Beaufort's estate in Gloucestershire in 1860. Not only have dramatic changes taken place over the whole of this period but, more importantly, significant changes have taken place over

the last 20 years. When I first played for England in 1968 I used a wooden-headed racket with a chrome-plated steel shaft, strung in natural gut. The weight of this racket was around 120g/ 4oz. While such a style of racket allowed the player to perform a wide range of strokes it was a lot more

sluggish through the air, and powerful shots demanded an emphatic swing. The modern competition racket is around 25% lighter than the wooden-headed racket and weighs 90 - 95g / 3½oz. In addition to the reduced weight, a balance point of around 29/30cm/12in from the end of the handle produces a racket that is much faster through the air. The player can now make rapier-like movements with very little backswing, and with the reduced reaction time necessary to play a stroke, the resulting exchange of shots can be very fast indeed. To produce such a finely balanced light-weight implement new materials have been used. The new rackets fall largely into one of two categories.

The two-piece racket

These are made by joining a light-weight drawn-aluminium-tube head to a shaft by means of a zinc alloy, die-cast T-piece. The shaft itself is prefer-ably made of graphite fibres as these are strong yet light and provide a powerful recoil when the shaft bends in use.

Steel shafts are still commonly used but these are usually graphite coated or painted to reduce the weight from the former, heavy, chrome-plated alternative. The shaft is secured with a non-slip synthetic grip. Wooden handles vary in weight, being of natural material, and consequently it is difficult to produce any two rackets exactly the same in weight and balance. Also, because wood is a rigid material, the movement of the shaft is restricted, thereby limiting its power-producing recoil. For these reasons the extended shaft and more flexible cork- or foam-handled rackets have evolved. The greater recoil produces more power with the same degree of effort. Because the stress points at the top of the handle have been removed more flexible shafts can be used which best suit certain styles of play. Generally speaking flexible shafts are more powerful whereas stiff shafts offer the maximum degree of control of the shuttle.

One-piece rackets

These rackets are moulded under temperature and pressure using a combination of graphite fibres and a thermosetting resin. Graphite fibres have tremendous tensile strength and are very light. When they are matrixed the torsion of twisting is reduced almost entirely and the resulting racket is lightweight yet of high strength.

Below: The modern one-piece graphite racket.

Bottom: The shaft of this one-piece racket extends to its full length. The grip, of cork bound with synthetic leather, is moulded onto the shaft.

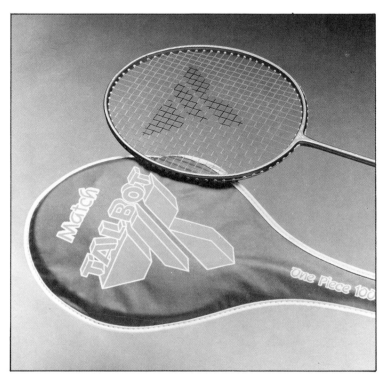

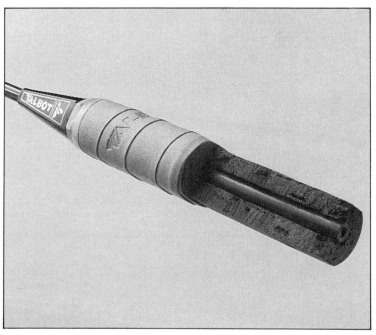

Additives can be combined with the base material to obtain special properties. Boron is used for extra strength and lightness. Kevlar is a high modulus additive which has vibration dampening properties, whilst ceramic additives are more forgiving and flexible. One-piece rackets can be fitted with wooden handles or moulded over the total length of the racket and fitted with a lightweight grip. The popularity of these rackets has continued even though they are more susceptible to breakage when in a collision of rackets.

Racket strings

Stringing choice is vast with tremendous development in the world of synthetic strings. While few would deny the superb playability of natural gut many players are turning to synthetic strings to give them higher tension and greater durability.

Natural gut has been developed so that it can be virtually impervious to changes in temperature and humidity. Nevertheless, the progress of synthetic strings has been equally impressive, particularly with the use of multifilament and matrixed constructions. High-melting-point materials make the job of stringing easier as the strings don't burn across one another when pulled through the frame. Early synthetic strings, usually of monofilament construction, stretched and lost tension. The modern-day equivalents can maintain high tension with the minimum of stretch.

Below: A selection of badminton rackets used in times gone by — a far cry from today's light-weight moulded carbon rackets.

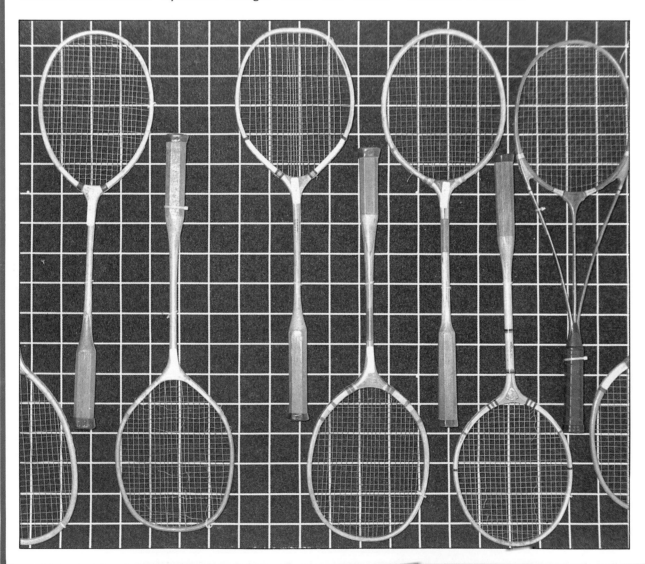

Left: Shoes for sport answer a great many requirements: lightness, good support, flexibility and good grip.

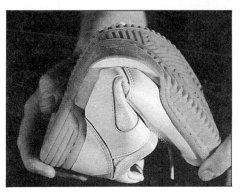

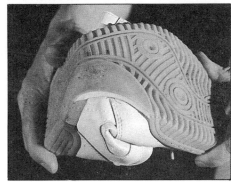

Far left: Flexibility is of great importance because of the speed of movement and changes of direction that badminton demands.

Left: It should be possible to twist as well as bend a badminton shoe. The sole shows a special gripping section to improve floor contact.

Suitable footwear is particularly important and there are a number of factors which should be looked for when purchasing a new pair of shoes. Firstly, flexibility of the sole is necessary to allow full foot movement and yet the sole and inner sole should be good shock absorbers. Both foot and heel strikes occur in badminton and, unless the shock of such impact is absorbed, injury to the joints particularly is likely. If the sole is too rigid a twisted ankle could result from the rocking motion necessary for sideways movement or a sudden change of direction. Secondly, a good grip is required to cope with the variability of court surface. Lastly, you need a breathable upper which also offers support and stability for the foot and ankle.

Clothing

You should wear predominantly white clothes. Vanity has its place but clothing must be comfortable, loose fitting and unrestricting over the range of movements involved. Cushioned socks can help prevent blisters. A most important item of clothing for the well-being of the player is a tracksuit. This is essential to keep the muscles warm during the warm-up and warm-down exercises. Personal preferences may differ but a cotton lining next to the skin is an ideal, comfortable, yet breathable material.

The shuttlecock and net

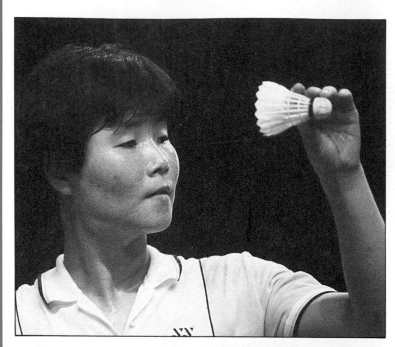

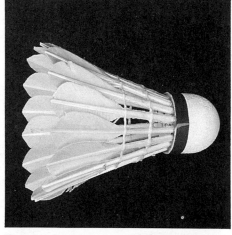

Above: Hwang Hye-Young of Korea about to serve. Concentration and balance at the point of service are important for accuracy and deception.

Right: Shuttlecocks made of feathers (top) and moulded nylon (below). The development of the nylon shuttlecock has helped the growth in popularity of the game.

Opposite: Darren Hall of Great Britain plays a whip shot at the net.

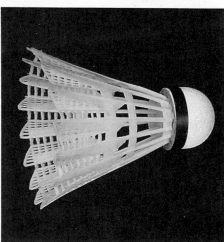

The shuttlecock is a unique object in that its flight path is so very different from that of a ball. The sudden steepening of its trajectory make the shuttle difficult to 'time' in play and is against all the natural coordination that people develop as children playing with a ball. Its construction throughout most of the life of the sport has been of feathers in a kid covered cork base. These feathers are preferably those from the tail of the goose and the very best feathers are the straight ones from the centre of the tail. It takes several geese to produce sufficient feathers necessary for a top grade shuttlecock and consequently sheer economics has brought about the development and extensive use of the nylon shuttlecock. The skirt of the nylon shuttle is injection moulded and can be fitted to a synthetic or cork base. The immense development of the sport at grass roots level in schools and sports centres depended very much on a budget shuttle and the nylon fulfils this need.

However, cheaper feathered shuttlecocks are available to the market, made either from bent goose feathers or less expensive duck feathers. There is undoubtedly a need for nylon shuttlecocks but I have no doubt that the skill level achievable with feathered shuttles is very much higher than with nylon, because of the manner in which the feathers grip the strings. This allows the player greater control with slicing actions. Also nylon shuttlecocks do have a habit of 'folding' when smashed severely, increasing the pace of the shuttle to such a level that a controlled return is almost impossible.

A variety of string-like materials including nylon are used in nets, but preferably they should be of 2cm/$\frac{3}{4}$" square mesh so that shuttles struck against the net do not stick into the mesh. Fine rope is the best material to support the net over the posts as wire, which is sometimes used, may deflect the path of shuttles which clip the tape.

Facilities

Badminton has great popularity because a court of this size can be laid out in most sports halls, gymnasiums, school halls, drill halls and other public covered places.

Ceiling height
Perhaps the main consideration is the height of the hall, which should be a minimum of 10m/32′ 6″ for ideal conditions. Nevertheless, the game can be enjoyed even if the hall is as low as 7m/22′ 9″.

Floor surface
A sprung wooden floor such as maple provides the perfect playing surface. However, great progress has been made in recent years with synthetic surfaces and many sports halls are now fitted with floor surfaces which provide good friction yet are not 'sticky'. Floors which provide too good a grip can cause injury when the player attempts a sudden change in direction. The synthetic surfaces tend to have good shock absorption properties and are therefore preferable to the hard floors found in many multi-purpose sports-halls. These hard surfaces have a harmful effect on joints and knee injuries are a common problem.

Architects responsible for the design of multi-purpose sports halls have not generally had the best interests of badminton in mind particularly when it comes to background colour and lighting. Walls are frequently white whereas a pastel colour, preferably green or blue, would provide a background which would allow the player to see the shuttle clearly during play. Deception is so much easier in a hall with an inappropriate background.

Lighting
Another important factor is the quality and type of lighting and here again some halls have their lights positioned so that they distract players who look

Below: A modern badminton hall with excellent conditions. Lighting, background, floor, floor markings create the right ambience for an enjoyable game.

up to follow the flight path of the shuttle. Lights positioned out of court down each of the two sides of the court are preferable. In such a position the higher the intensity the better as light reflects off the white shuttle, offering the player a clear image, and provides the best possible chance of perfect timing of strokes. Perhaps the best lighting conditions are those provided by the television companies who need high intensity light to produce a clear picture on the screen. Many sports are adversely affected by TV lights but not badminton, which is why the very highest standard of play can be seen on television.

All these requirements for perfect conditions are possible and indeed purpose-built facilities are on the increase worldwide. In Copenhagen alone there are more than 50 purpose-built badminton halls, which is almost 10 times as many as in the whole of the UK. Little wonder Denmark has boasted so many world class players and why the game is second only to football in terms of status and popularity. Let us hope that other countries will follow Denmark's example and provide for the huge number of participants a greater number of purpose-built facilities for both general enjoyment and the development of world-class players.

Above: Top competition conditions for the English National Badminton Championships include television lighting which most players enjoy.

15

Chapter 2 **The Rules of the Game**

Badminton is a game for singles (two players) or doubles (four players). The opponents play on opposite sides of a court with a net between them. The object of the game is to hit a shuttle with a racket across the net so that it will land within the opponent's court but out of his reach; or to force the opponent to hit the shuttle out of court or into the net. Either tactic achieved by the server or his partner wins a point; either tactic achieved by the receiver or his partner means a change of service. The first side to score the right number of points wins the game. There are three games in a match.

Below: A classic mixed doubles formation in a big match.

Doubles

Doubles can be 'even' — two men or two women opposing a similar pair — or 'mixed' — each pair comprising a man and a woman.

Players toss to decide positions and order of service before beginning the game. One player spins a coin and a member of the other side calls 'heads' or 'tails'. When the coin falls, the winner of the toss can make one of two choices: who serves first or which end to play. The opponents take the second choice. The service couple are 'in' and the receivers 'out'.

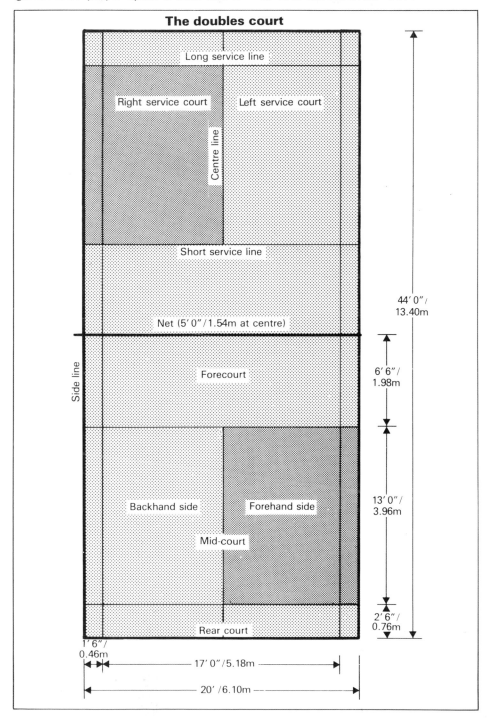

The doubles court

Long service line

Right service court

Left service court

Centre line

Short service line

Net (5' 0" / 1.54m at centre)

Side line

Forecourt

Backhand side

Forehand side

Mid-court

Rear court

44' 0" / 13.40m

6' 6" / 1.98m

13' 0" / 3.96m

2' 6" / 0.76m

1' 6" / 0.46m

17' 0" / 5.18m

20' / 6.10m

Singles

Singles is played as for doubles, except that the tramlines at the side of the court are out-of-bounds. However, the service court extends right to the back of the court, to the very base line.

So that the server may serve from both sides of his end of court, service is delivered from the right-hand side when the server's score is 0 or an even number, and from the left-hand court when the score has reached an odd number.

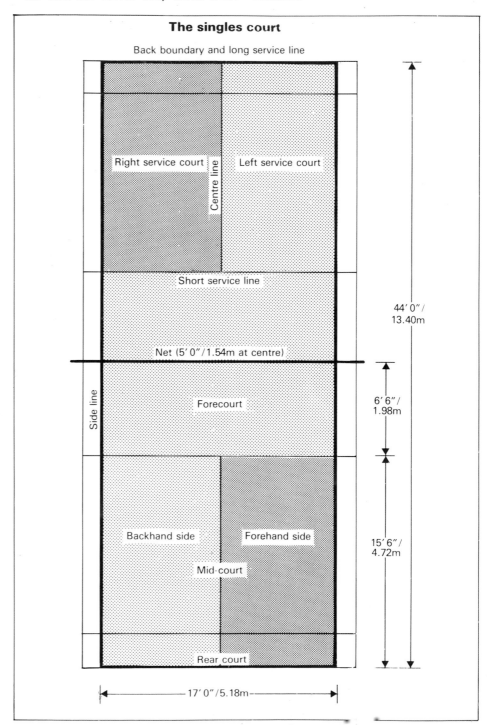

The singles court

Back boundary and long service line

Right service court

Centre line

Left service court

Short service line

Net (5' 0"/1.54m at centre)

Side line

Forecourt

Backhand side

Forehand side

Mid-court

Rear court

44' 0" / 13.40m

6' 6" / 1.98m

15' 6" / 4.72m

17' 0"/5.18m

The service

The first service is delivered from the right-hand service court, diagonally opposite into the receiver's right-hand court. The receiver should keep within the bounds of the service court and his feet should not touch the line until the shuttle has been hit, or a fault will be called. The centre line counts as 'in court' if the shuttle lands on it, and all the lines count as 'in' the area they enclose. The rules of service are:

1 The server must wait until the receiver is ready. Neither side should hold up play with delaying tactics.

2 The server should stand within the appropriate service court, which changes according to the score.

3 The server should have both feet touching the ground until the shuttle has been hit.

4 The shuttle should be below the server's waist as it is struck.

5 When the shuttle is struck, the head of the racket should be below the hand holding the grip.

6 The shuttle must be hit over the net into the service court diagonally opposite.

7 It is not permitted to feign a service in order to deceive the opponent.

8 If one of the above rules is broken, a fault is called against the server who must relinquish service.

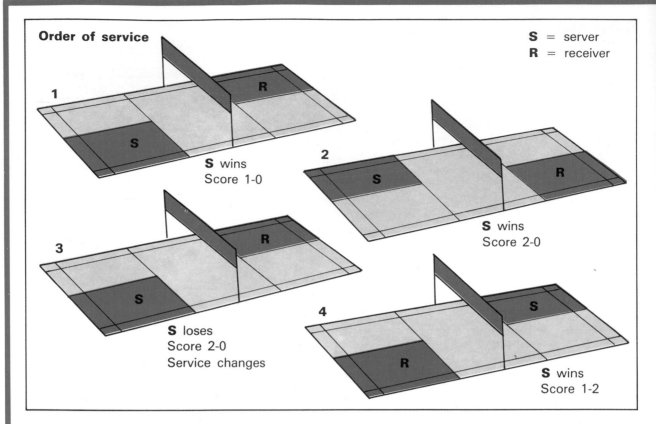

Order of service

S = server
R = receiver

1 S wins
Score 1-0

2 S wins
Score 2-0

3 S loses
Score 2-0
Service changes

4 S wins
Score 1-2

Order of service

The chosen server begins the match and hits the shuttle into the diagonally opposite service court. If the server's side wins the rally, the same player will serve again, but the serving partners change sides. The receivers remain in position. The same player serves from alternate sides of his end of court, and the receivers remain in position, until the serving side loses a rally. The service now passes to the opposition, to the player in the right-hand court. The players who have lost service go back to their original positions.

The new server now follows the pattern described above. If his side wins the rally, he and his partner change service courts, and he serves diagonally to his left. When the server's side loses a rally, the service changes again, but this time the server gives the shuttle to his partner. The serving pair commence play from where they were standing at the beginning of the rally just lost. The new server now serves from alternate sides until he loses a rally, when the service passes to the opposite pair, to the player who started in the right-hand court.

Thus the service passes round each player in turn, both partners on one side having an innings before the service passes to the opposition, to the player who started in the right-hand court. The exception is with the first service, which, once lost, passes directly to the opposition.

Receiving service

The receiver is the player standing diagonally opposite the server. He must stand within the service court and his feet should not touch the lines. He can stand anywhere within this area. He should aim to return a service that is good — where the shuttle will fall within the service court, including on the lines — to anywhere within the opponent's court, preferably to a position the opponent cannot reach, or where it will force him to commit a fault. If the receiver judges that the service will be out of court, he lets the shuttle hit the floor. If it is in court, the service passes to the opponent.

Scoring

Points can be scored only by the server and his partner winning a rally. If the receiving side wins the rally, the service passes to the next player, but the receivers do not score. The first side to score 15 points wins the game, though the target may also be set at 21 points or, in the case of ladies' singles, 11 points. The first side to win two games wins the match. Sides change ends after the first game, after the second game if there is to be a third,

and during the third game when the score has been tipped in favour of one side or the other, ie when one side reaches 6 in a game of 11, 8 in a game of 15, or 11 in a game of 21.

Losing a rally

A player commits a fault and the rally is lost if:

1 The server misses the shuttle in trying to deliver service.

2 A player catches the shuttle on his

Below: In this men's doubles match the score for each side is displayed on the automatic courtside scoreboard.

racket and then slings it instead of hitting it.

3 A player does not manage to return the shuttle over the net into the opponent's court.

4 A player hits the shuttle twice instead of returning it with one hit.

5 A player and his partner both hit the shuttle before it is returned over the net.

6 A player allows the shuttle to touch the floor before hitting it.

7 During play, a player touches the net or its supports with his person, clothes or racket.

8 A player hits the shuttle before it has flown over the net. (It is permissible to follow a shot across the net with the racket, provided the net is not touched.)

9 A player touches the shuttle with his person or clothes.

10 A player obstructs an opponent by wielding a racket under the net, throwing a racket, or other disruptive or distracting behaviour.

Lets

A rally may be interrupted by a let without either side scoring an advantage.

1 A let may be called by the receiver if the server has won a point but served from the wrong side, or by the server if the receivers stood in the wrong position and won a rally. Let must be called immediately the rally in question is over, or it is not valid. If a let is called too late, the game proceeds with no adjustment to scoring and players remain in their adopted positions.

2 A let may be called if there is an accidental interruption to play, such as interference from another court or if the shuttle gets hooked in the net after dropping over it.

3 Since 1958 there has been no service let. If the shuttle strikes the top of the net and still lands in the diagonally opposite service court, the shot is good. If the shuttle strikes the top of the net and lands outside the service area, that is a fault.

When to set a game

This is similar to 'deuce' in tennis, ie when the score is level near the end of the game. Setting is a way of prolonging the game to regain a lost advantage when a side has come within a point or two of winning and then loses the service, with the result that the other side catches up and has the advantage. The side that first reached the higher score can 'set' the game, which means that the score reverts to 0-0 ('love-all'), and the first side to win 2, 3 or 5 points wins the game.

To give an example: side A leads by 14 points to 12 in a 15-point game. Side B regains the serve and levels the score at 14-all. Because A was the first to reach 14, that side now has the option of setting the game. They decide to do so to cancel out the distinct advantage that server B now holds — at least two chances of winning the match, one for each partner serving. The score reverts to 0-0 and the first side to win 3 points claims the game.

The game may be set at two points, as shown on the table below. Players may call to set at only the appropriate points. Setting is not allowed in handicapped games.

Scores needed to set a game		
Points needed to win the game	Score when game may be set	Points needed to win after setting
11	9-all	3
11	10-all	2
15	13-all	5
15	14-all	3
21	19-all	5
21	20-all	3

Chapter 3 **Fitness and Training**

Richard Harmsworth improves his stamina and strength by including running in his training schedule. Legs need to work hard in badminton but a training programme should be balanced and designed to incorporate exercises for all the body.

Players of differing standards often ask how they can become better players. A straightforward reply would be to 'keep practising' but perhaps a more pertinent reply, particularly to club standard players, would be to say 'do some badminton training'.

Fitness is very individualized, is specific to the game, is probably the easiest aspect in which to make progress — but it is often neglected.

It is important to prepare well ahead of the start of each season, leaving time to polish up racket skills before matches and tournaments start. Last minute efforts are of limited value as the human body responds slowly and needs time to consolidate mental and physiological adaptations. It is easy to return to a previously achieved standard with a reasonable amount of training, but a concentrated effort of six to eight weeks is needed to lift that standard to a higher plane.

Modern sport is concerned with speed and aggression. Badminton is no exception and fast play over a long period of time can be very exhausting. This makes fitness essential, preferably leaving some energy in hand over your opponent's level of fitness to concentrate on stokes and tactics.

Singles

Singles play requires considerable athletic ability. Stamina, speed and strength, added to the skills of the game, are needed to answer pressure created by an opponent's shots while still leaving capacity for effective replies.

Doubles

Doubles is faster but over shorter distances with a faster striking rate, faster leg work and quicker thinking to maintain control of the rallies and force winning shots.

The need for work

If you are a naturally gifted player you will achieve some success but will become limited at the higher levels unless you are willing to work at the game. A healthy human being responds readily to an 'overload' system. When made to work quite hard, the body will recover and *add* to its resources — it over-compensates, so that the same workload will be easier next time. In a sporting activity, this means that more work can be tolerated. It is a 'stepping-up' system: we get fitter to get fitter.

The five S's

A training programme is vital, planned in a sequence allowing several weeks for substantial effect. The key to success in badminton as indeed for all racket sports is known as the five S's — stamina, strength, suppleness, speed and (p)sychology.

Stamina

It is easy to get a base level of fitness or stamina by running regularly which also helps to build up cardiovascular fitness. When you start, run on alternate days, so your legs can adjust. Run for at least 20 minutes slowly, building up on time and distance. Spend a short period of time in practising running backwards which is particularly useful for singles players.

Strength

Running up hills is a particularly good way of strengthening leg muscles, as is running in soft sand. As progress is made, you should eventually be able to 'attack' the hills by sprinting.

Exercise can be arranged into a circuit, aimed mainly at the legs but including some arm work and abdominal and back exercises. Your back and stomach muscles need to be

Right: Weight-training with the help of modern equipment helps to concentrate on strengthening specific muscles. On the right Richard Harmsworth is exercising the biceps.

strengthened to form a solid link between strong, hard-working legs and your striking arm. Circuit training is a very efficient form of strengthening. It is, perhaps, better carried out in a group and can also be done to music. Many exercises can be incorporated — skipping, bar jumping, sit ups, press ups, squat thrusts, step ups, hopping, tuck jumps to name but a few.

Another excellent way to increase strength is an organized weight training programme. The main properties of muscle are strength, endurance, speed, co-ordination and flexibility. Such a programme is concerned with improving the first three of these (the other two being covered by pure badminton play and stretching exercises).

'Heavy weight — low repetition' work will strengthen muscles, thereby adding power to attacking strokes, and making muscles less prone to injury. More important, however, is the fact that 'heavy weight — low repetition' work performed at high speed will develop particularly the fast twitch muscle fibres, thereby increasing the speed the muscles can work. It is for this reason that, during the playing season, slow lifting of heavy weights should be avoided, because the effect of this type of work is more suitable for body builders, who aim to achieve large muscle bulk.

Finally, 'light weight — high repetition' work can be used to improve endurance. The advantage of weights as a method of achieving fitness is that they can be applied to any selected group of muscles and progress can be recorded as resistance and the number of repetitions is increased.

If you are unsure about how to approach this type of training, it is better to seek expert advice. Health and fitness clubs, where qualified instructors are only too willing to help and advise, are an ideal location.

Above: The quadriceps (thigh) muscles are being strengthened by pushing them together against the weights counter-balanced on the training equipment.

Suppleness

One fundamental in a game where opponents are often trying to put the shuttle out of reach is suppleness or flexibility. Quick, twisting movements are needed and explosive actions dominate. Stretching must, therefore, become part of training and playing procedures, not only before work begins, but preceding and following any activity which puts your muscles under stress.

The importance of warming-up cannot be over emphasized because cold, tight muscles are more likely to be injured. The amateur player often ignores the warm-up even though it can be completed in a few minutes. As you become fitter you can increase the time spent on the warm-up. Do the exercises smoothly (see page 43), increasing your range and the vigour of the movement as you feel the large muscle groups limbering up. Never force a movement — gradually push yourself a little further on each repetition. As well as loosening and limbering, these exercises raise the pulse rate and the muscles are signalled that they are about to be stretched and worked.

Speed

This takes the form of faster runs with a rest between the runs (interval running). Run forwards and backwards over distances of 50-200 metres.

For example (after a warm-up and stretching):

1 Sprint 100 metres, jog back to start, repeat and build up the number of repetitions.

2 Sprint 50 metres backwards, walk back to start and repeat.

3 If training with a group of players, form teams of three and run continuous shuttle relays over a variety of set distances, for a fixed period of time (say 5 minutes first, then 10, then 15).

A useful safety system is to run at 75% effort on the first relay to rehearse the task, and to prevent injury. Remember that with these three stages, training should be built up gradually — do not try too much too soon. After working hard *stretch* the muscles put under pressure to prevent stiffness.

4 Skip on your toes, emphasizing relaxed leg muscles, for continuous periods of 5 minutes. Once again build up slowly and increase with fitness to periods of 15 and 20 minutes without rest. Additional pressure can be applied by pretending periodically that you are playing in a fast rally and speed up the rate of skipping.

5 Certainly the hardest, and probably the best, method is that of 'multi-shuttle feeds', which is a game-related exercise. This can be done at club night with players in groups of three (one worker, two feeders). The idea here is to get used to playing at a far greater speed than is possible in a game situation. The feeders have 10 to 15 shuttles each and as the first shuttle is played, the second is fed, then a third and so on with the feeders feeding alternately. You should continue to play even if you miss or play a bad shot until the sequence is completed. It is important that the feeding is accurate and can be to a set pattern. Try the following sequence: (1) high lifts so that the worker can smash; (2) hand-fed shuttles around the net so that the worker can hit net shots and net kills; (3) a combination of these two.

(P)sychology

There are many factors which contribute to success on court. Approaching matches in the right frame of mind and with the determination to win is essential. This subject is covered in greater detail in Chapter 7 on page 124.

Players show this determination in different ways. Opponents must feel the weight of the players' competitive drive, the relentless pressure, the refusal to be beaten, the *inner strength* facing them. In close matches between well-balanced opponents, the will to win will decide the outcome.

The right frame of mind and good sportsmanship are linked. Exceptions can be quoted but in general the better players or 'true champions' will over-

Left: Stretching exercises improve suppleness and aid players when reaching for shuttlecocks, and in their quest to satisfy the complex footwork of the game.

come the pressures in the game and remain calm and courteous throughout. It may not always be easy, but part of training is learning to keep calm under pressure, keeping your mind working positively, and keeping the skills together, rather than letting emotions wreck them.

Training

Slow stretching exercises aim to extend the muscles at any particular joint or part of the body. The stretching helps to increase your range of movement, or flexibility. This helps general movement in play and improves your capacity to play harder, lessen the risk of injury and help you to recover quickly after hard exercise. After each exercise, shake out — loosely shake your limbs to release any muscle tension that may have built up during exercise.

When you train, your body does more than just adapt to the extra load you are placing on it — it over-compensates so that you can handle even greater loads, if necessary. In this way you can gradually improve with a sustained training programme.

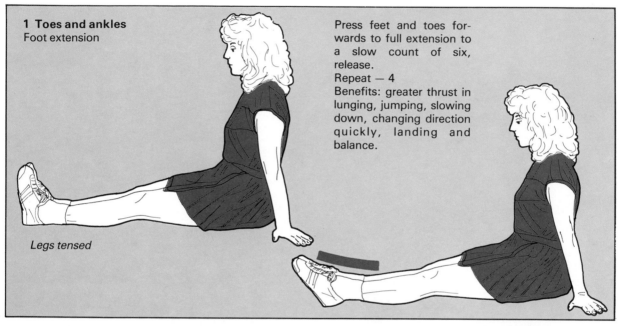

1 Toes and ankles
Foot extension

Legs tensed

Press feet and toes for-wards to full extension to a slow count of six, release.
Repeat — 4
Benefits: greater thrust in lunging, jumping, slowing down, changing direction quickly, landing and balance.

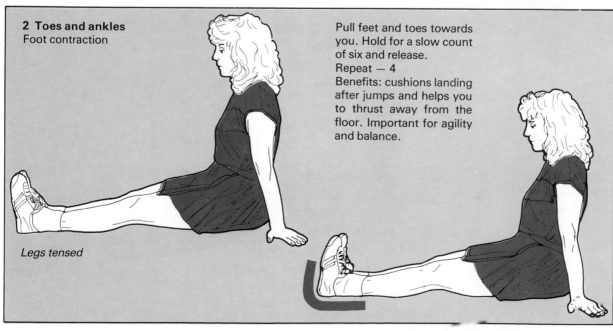

2 Toes and ankles
Foot contraction

Legs tensed

Pull feet and toes towards you. Hold for a slow count of six and release.
Repeat — 4
Benefits: cushions landing after jumps and helps you to thrust away from the floor. Important for agility and balance.

3 Knees and hips
Alternate leg raising

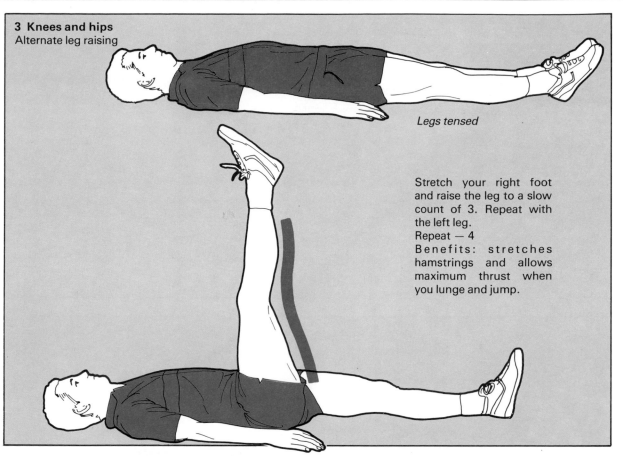

Legs tensed

Stretch your right foot and raise the leg to a slow count of 3. Repeat with the left leg.
Repeat — 4
Benefits: stretches hamstrings and allows maximum thrust when you lunge and jump.

4 Knees and hips
Knee to chest contraction

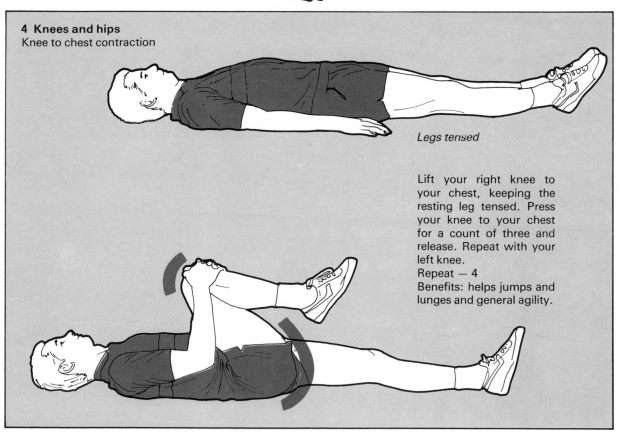

Legs tensed

Lift your right knee to your chest, keeping the resting leg tensed. Press your knee to your chest for a count of three and release. Repeat with your left knee.
Repeat — 4
Benefits: helps jumps and lunges and general agility.

5 Hip joints
Knee presses

Sit on the floor

Holding your feet, press your knees towards the floor with your elbows.
Hold for a count of 6 and release.
Repeat — 4
Benefits: greater flexibility in lunging. Aids recovery.

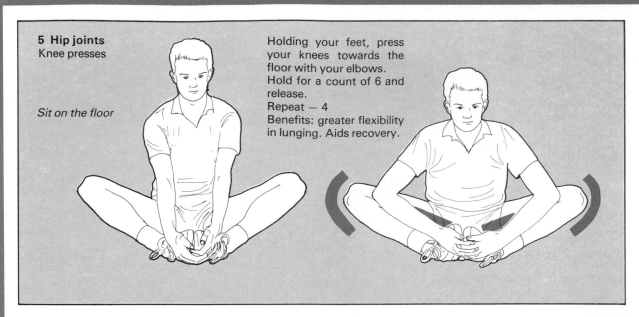

6 Lower back, hips, knees and shoulders
Back extension

Slide your hands down your shins, and drop your head towards your knees. Reach towards your toes, keeping your legs tensed. Hold for a count of six and release.
Repeat — 4

Legs tensed

Benefits: greater flexibility for stretching out for shuttles during play.

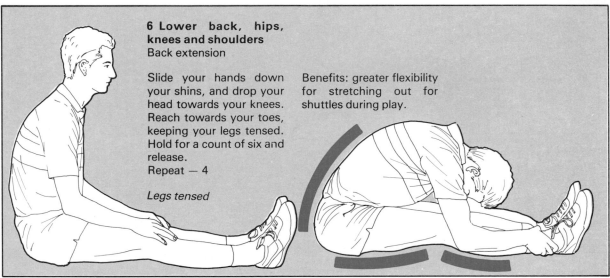

7 Lower back, hips, knees and shoulders
Back and leg extension

Slide your hands forwards on the floor between your legs, with your legs as far apart as possible. Hold for a count of six and release.
Repeat — 4

Legs tensed

Benefits: greater stretch in side and forward lunges, and backward scissors jumps to the rear court.

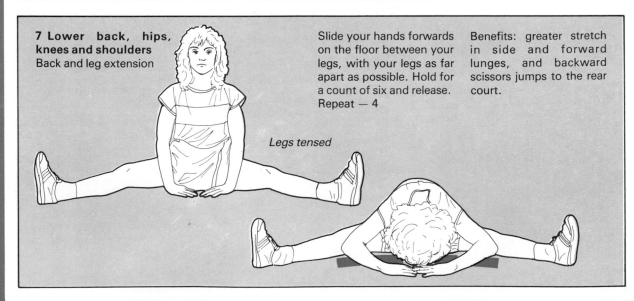

8 Sides, lower back, hips, knees and shoulders
Side and leg extension

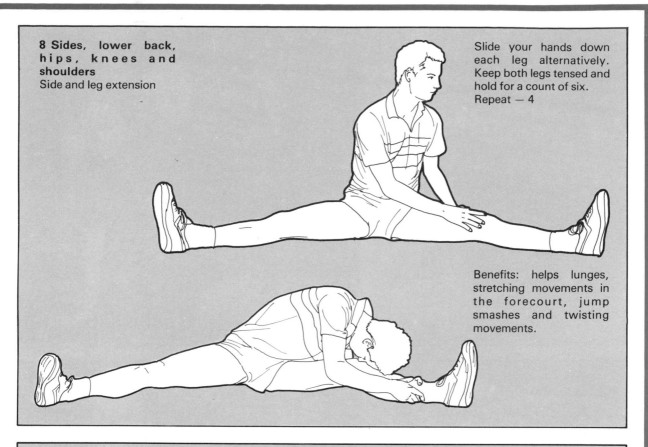

Slide your hands down each leg alternatively. Keep both legs tensed and hold for a count of six.
Repeat — 4

Benefits: helps lunges, stretching movements in the forecourt, jump smashes and twisting movements.

9 Back, hips and knees
Hurdle stretches

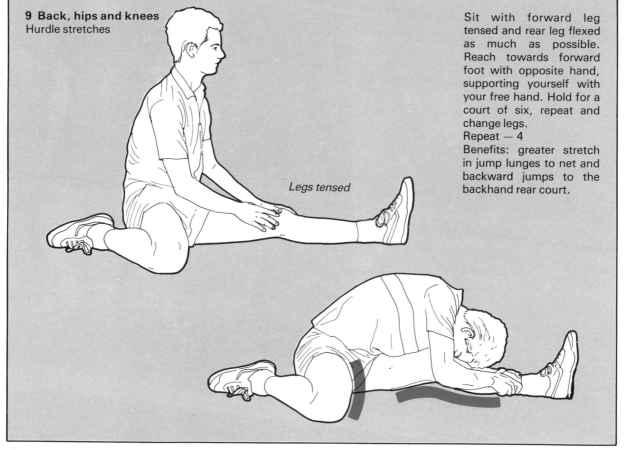

Legs tensed

Sit with forward leg tensed and rear leg flexed as much as possible. Reach towards forward foot with opposite hand, supporting yourself with your free hand. Hold for a court of six, repeat and change legs.
Repeat — 4
Benefits: greater stretch in jump lunges to net and backward jumps to the backhand rear court.

10 Hips and chest
Back arches

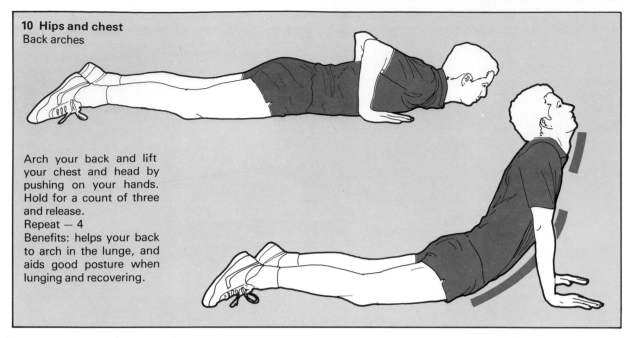

Arch your back and lift your chest and head by pushing on your hands. Hold for a count of three and release.
Repeat — 4
Benefits: helps your back to arch in the lunge, and aids good posture when lunging and recovering.

11 Knees and ankles
Pliés and pushes

Keeping your feet flat on the floor, lower your knees over your toes for a count of three. Straighten legs slowly.
Repeat — 4

Benefits: helps jumps, lunges, landings and recovery; general agility and speed; balance and posture.

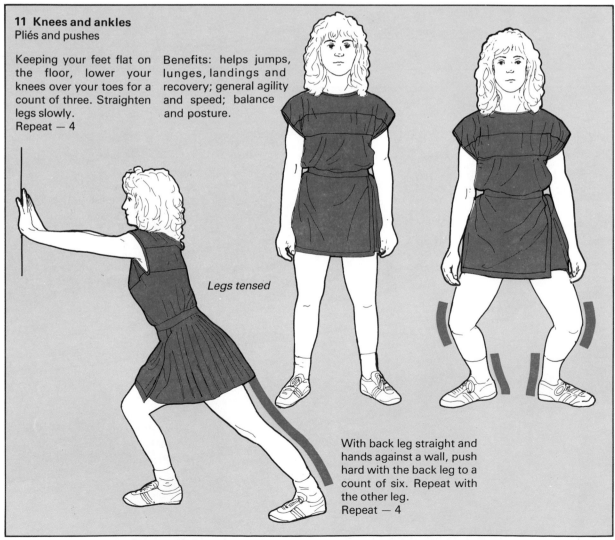

Legs tensed

With back leg straight and hands against a wall, push hard with the back leg to a count of six. Repeat with the other leg.
Repeat — 4

12 Ankles
Body raising

With both feet flat on the floor, raise your body by extending your feet until you are well balanced on your toes. Hold for a count of 3 and lower your heels.

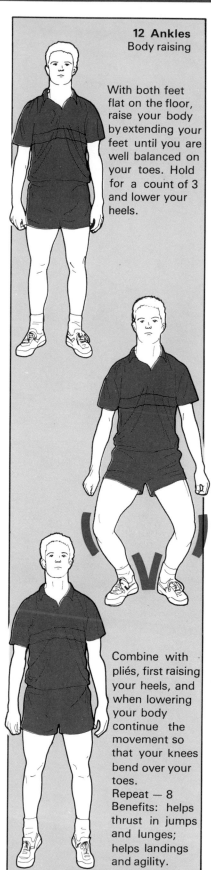

Combine with pliés, first raising your heels, and when lowering your body continue the movement so that your knees bend over your toes.
Repeat — 8
Benefits: helps thrust in jumps and lunges; helps landings and agility.

13 Ankles and knees
Jumps

Lower your body in a plié and thrust upwards into a jump. Land softly and bend your knees in a plié.
Repeat — 8

Benefits: helps to develop power to trust away from the floor; helps landing and balance.

14 Ankles and knees
Jumps

Lower your body further in the plié and jump. While jumping first thrust the feet out to the side and then back together.
Repeat — 8

Benefits: helps to develop power to trust away from the floor; helps landing and balance.

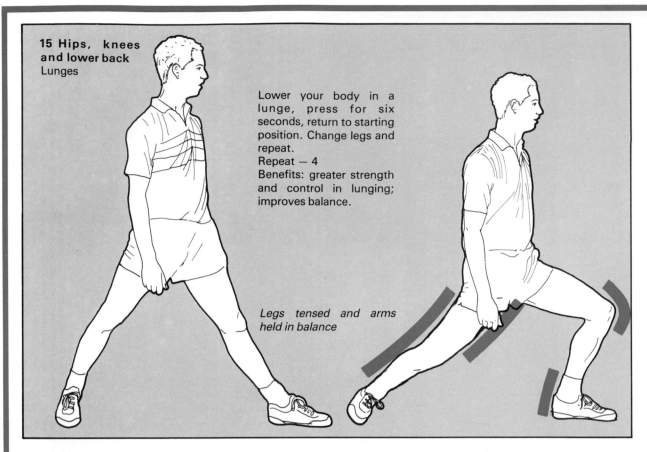

15 Hips, knees and lower back
Lunges

Lower your body in a lunge, press for six seconds, return to starting position. Change legs and repeat.
Repeat — 4
Benefits: greater strength and control in lunging; improves balance.

Legs tensed and arms held in balance

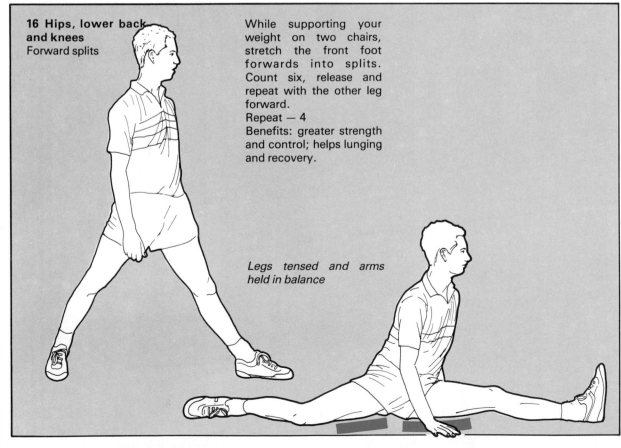

16 Hips, lower back and knees
Forward splits

While supporting your weight on two chairs, stretch the front foot forwards into splits. Count six, release and repeat with the other leg forward.
Repeat — 4
Benefits: greater strength and control; helps lunging and recovery.

Legs tensed and arms held in balance

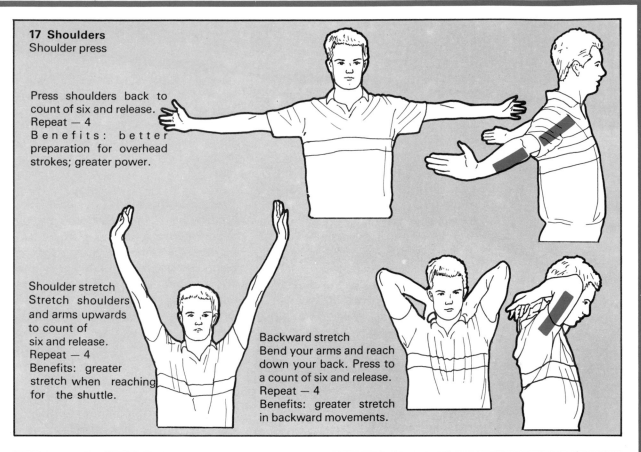

17 Shoulders
Shoulder press

Press shoulders back to count of six and release. Repeat — 4
Benefits: better preparation for overhead strokes; greater power.

Shoulder stretch
Stretch shoulders and arms upwards to count of six and release. Repeat — 4
Benefits: greater stretch when reaching for the shuttle.

Backward stretch
Bend your arms and reach down your back. Press to a count of six and release. Repeat — 4
Benefits: greater stretch in backward movements.

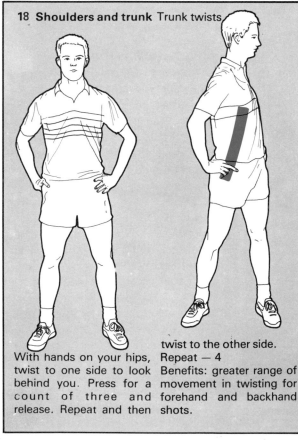

18 Shoulders and trunk Trunk twists

With hands on your hips, twist to one side to look behind you. Press for a count of three and release. Repeat and then twist to the other side. Repeat — 4
Benefits: greater range of movement in twisting for forehand and backhand shots.

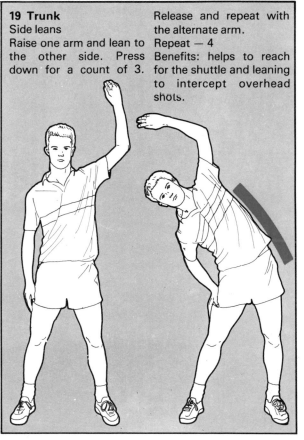

19 Trunk
Side leans
Raise one arm and lean to the other side. Press down for a count of 3. Release and repeat with the alternate arm. Repeat — 4
Benefits: helps to reach for the shuttle and leaning to intercept overhead shots.

Diet

It is all very well keeping yourself active and well exercised, but how can you be sure that you and your body machine are getting the right nourishment.

The right balance

Your food should balance your body's needs for:

Nutrients (proteins, fats, carbohydrate, vitamins, minerals and water) — the raw materials needed to build and repair the body machine;

Energy (calories) — to power the body machine and all the thousands of different mechanisms and actions that keep you alive and active;

Dietary fibre (a complex mixture of natural plant substances including what was once called 'roughage') — lack of fibre seems to be connected with many body disorders and is the single most important form of food likely to be lacking in your everyday diet.

Body management

Management of body composition should combine diet and exercise to achieve the optimum energy balance between calories in (food) and calories out (exercise) while meeting the nutritional needs of the body.

Virtually everything you eat contains energy — measured as calories. The higher a food's calorie rating, the more energy it supplies. But don't make the mistake of thinking that eating extra energy-rich foods will make you more energetic. The amount of energy in your day-to-day diet should exactly balance the energy your body burns up. If you eat more than you use, the surplus energy is stored as body fat.

Eating before action

You should not depend on a pre-game meal as the energy source for tournament games, club matches or training sessions. Energy used during an event or workout comes from food consumed days prior to the event. The most significant consideration regarding a pre-game meal is that it should not interfere with the physiological stresses associated with athletic performance. The pre-game meal should consist of items that you like and find acceptable.

Individual differences must be taken into account. However, there are guidelines that can serve as a starting point until you find the pre-game meal that works best.

Your stomach should be empty before you play. This will help prevent competition between the stomach and muscles for the blood supply. A pre-game meal two to three hours before a

---

Increasing fibre intake

A healthy diet should contain between 30-40 grams of fibre per day. Each of the following foods contains 10 grams of fibre. By adding some of these to your daily diet, you can increase your fibre intake.

35g/1¼oz All Bran
4½ wholewheat breakfast biscuits
120g/4¼oz wholemeal break
300g/11oz wholewheat pasta, cooked
240g/8¼oz broad beans, boiled
400g/14oz potatoes, unpeeled
120g/4½oz red kidney beans, cooked
350g/12¼oz carrots
680g/1½lb oranges
40g/1½oz dried apricots
150g/5oz sultanas
370g/13oz cabbage.

Other high-fibre foods are baked beans, lentils, brown rice, apples, prunes, peas, sweetcorn and wholegrain cereals. Eating more of these in place of meat will automatically increase your fibre intake.

match is ideal. For most this will allow ample time for the stomach to empty. Liquid pre-game meals can be consumed closer to competition time as these will leave the stomach faster than solid foods.

There are some factors relating to the composition of foods that should be taken into account. Fats remain in the stomach longer than carbohydrates and proteins. Carbohydrates are very quickly digested and readily absorbed. Therefore, a pre-game meal that is low in fat and adequate in carbohydrates is recommended.

In our sport, players are often required to compete in several games over a prolonged period of time, with rest breaks of varying lengths, particularly in tournament situations. On such days eating is always a problem. Carbohydrates that a player likes, taken in small amounts throughout the day, can ward off hunger, provide needed calories and help maintain adequate blood sugar levels.

More important than the need for food on such days is the need for water and this should be consumed in liberal amounts throughout the day.

Above: A selection of healthy, nutritious food — an essential part of any fitness programme.

Talbot's tips

During a competition do not drink fizzy or syrupy drinks as they cause excess gas in the stomach or help produce phlegm in the throat. Plain water or glucose drinks are preferable.

I believe that the training of healthy children should never be so serious that a special diet is required providing the player seems to perform well on a normal balanced diet. It is however most important during competition to eat little and often and avoid any food intake immediately prior to play.

Injuries and treatment

Common injuries

Badminton is characterized by quick, explosive movements and quick twisting movements, which put particular stresses on knees, ankles, shoulders, calf muscles, thigh muscles and back muscles. Hard floors, slippery surfaces and different court textures can also contribute to injury problems.

The most common injuries associated with badminton affect the body's soft tissues (muscles, tendons and ligaments). The basic treatment for all soft tissue injuries is the same. It is necessary to first ensure that the injury is not more severe than it seems.

Strain This causes a sharp, sudden pain and tenderness on touching the injured spot, but movement of the part is not affected even though it may be a little painful.

Sprain This is more serious, and more painful. The ligaments that keep the joint stable may be stretched or partially torn loose, such as when you 'go over' on your ankle in a fall. Sometimes the bones may also be slightly damaged and an x-ray may be required to determine the extent of the injury.

General treatment

Rest, Ice, Compression, Elevation (RICE).

Rest is important as an early measure to ensure the injury does not worsen.

Ice should be applied to the injured area for approximately 20 minutes (wrap the ice in a cloth or bag to protect the skin). If there is no ice available water can be applied directly by holding the injury under a cold tap. Repeat every two hours. The cooling helps to constrict the small blood vessels inside the injury and stop further bleeding and bruising.

Compression. After ice, bandage the injured area firmly but not too tightly. This will help stop further bleeding and disperse swelling.

Elevation. Raising an injury will help drain it by gravity and should help reduced swelling and any pain. For instance, if your ankle is injured, lie down with your foot raised higher than your body, supported by cushions or by any other comfortable means.

Other injuries

Tennis elbow may be caused by gripping the racket too hard, or by using too thin a grip.
Treatment: RICE, anti-inflammatories.

Eye injuries can be sustained by a direct hit with the shuttle or even a partner's racket.
Treatment: Gently apply an ice-cold compress. Great care should be taken here and if there is loss of vision, double vision or blurred vision for more than two minutes or if bruising prevents the eyelids opening then hospital attention should be received.

Foot blisters are commonly caused by rubbing, usually from poorly fitting shoes.
Treatment: If full of fluid they should be drained and sealed. Ensure that the blistered area is kept clean to avoid infection. Burst the blister with a sterile needle and cover the whole area with plain (no lint) elastoplast tape.

Shin splints may be due to the muscle swelling, that always occurs with exercise, distending the fairly rigid compartment in which the muscle is constrained. If you ignore it, it will progress and could become chronic. They can be caused by playing on very hard surfaces. They are painful to touch just to the outer side of the boney ridge at the front of the shin. If the condition fails to settle, it may be that the pain is the result of a stress fracture and you should seek medical help.
Treatment: RICE, especially rest. Anti-inflammatory drugs.

Tubular elasticated bandages

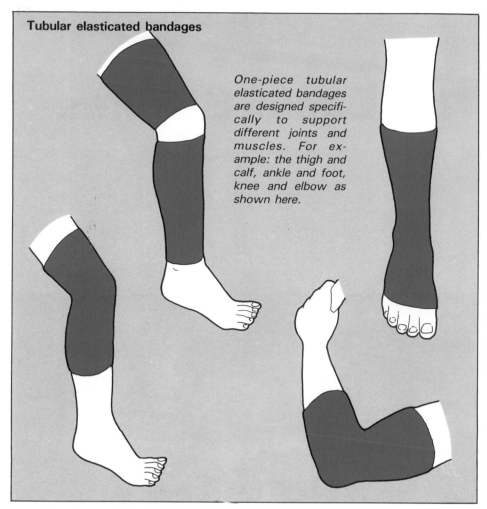

One-piece tubular elasticated bandages are designed specifically to support different joints and muscles. For example: the thigh and calf, ankle and foot, knee and elbow as shown here.

Knee and ankle injuries can be caused by poor technique. When reaching for a low shuttle place the trailing foot sideways.

Shoulder injuries can likewise be caused by poor technique such as using too much shoulder power in overhead smashes or taking shots face on rather than side on.

Returning after injury

After an injury it is important to get the injured part of the body back to full function and fitness. After 24 hours rest, *gently* start stretching the injured part and using it normally.

The more a recovering joint or muscle is exercised the better — do stretching exercises every hour or so, not just for a few minutes in the day. After 48 hours the injury should be well on the way to total recovery.

Finally a player can only be considered match fit if the following criteria can be satisfied:

1 There is an absence of swelling and pain.

2 If full power and flexibility has returned.

3 The player can jog for at least 20 minutes.

4 The player can execute short bursts of 50 metre sprints.

Talbot's tips

Injuries can create long periods of discomfort or indeed prevent healthy exercise altogether. Prevention of such injuries can be achieved by a thorough warm-up and warm-down (see page 43).

Chapter 4 The Basic Strokes

The warm-up

It is necessary for players of all standards to warm-up before playing in order to prevent injury. International players warm-up for more than 15 minutes, but three or four minutes of jogging, skipping or jumping on the spot is sufficient to increase your heart rate and the supply of oxygenated blood to your muscles, thereby raising your body temperature. Two or three minutes of general loosening exercises to stretch muscles will then ensure you are operating at the maximum range of flexibility of your joints. The following set of exercises provides a good warm-up (and warm-down) routine.

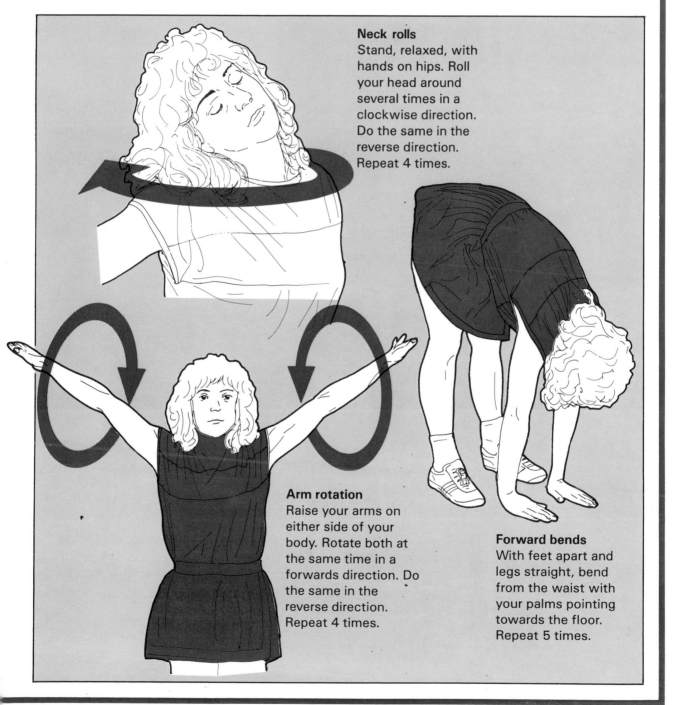

Neck rolls
Stand, relaxed, with hands on hips. Roll your head around several times in a clockwise direction. Do the same in the reverse direction. Repeat 4 times.

Arm rotation
Raise your arms on either side of your body. Rotate both at the same time in a forwards direction. Do the same in the reverse direction. Repeat 4 times.

Forward bends
With feet apart and legs straight, bend from the waist with your palms pointing towards the floor. Repeat 5 times.

Backward bends
Lock your hands together, bring them up and over your head, and bend backwards. Repeat 5 times.

Trunk curls
Hold your hands above your head. With feet apart roll your entire body around, firstly in a clockwise direction and then anticlockwise. Repeat 5 times.

Hip rotations
Place your hands on your hips. With feet apart roll your hips around, firstly in a clockwise direction, then anticlockwise. Repeat 5 times.

Knee bends
With feet a few inches apart, allowing your heels to raise, bend your knees fully. Repeat 5 times.

Squat stands
With your hands on your hips, and feet as far apart as possible, lower your body in a squat position as far as possible. Hold off for several seconds. Repeat 5 times.

Side squats
Stand with feet wide apart. Turn the upper part of your body, first to the left and then to the right. Bend the forward knee and hold for 5 seconds. Turn and bend the other knee, and hold for 5 seconds. Repeat 5 times.

Knee rotation
With feet together, bend and place your hands on your knees. Rotate your knees by pushing them out, then to one side, and then to the other, and continue in a fluid movement. Repeat in each direction 5 times.

Ankle rotation
Start with your toes on the floor, rotate your ankles as far as possible, in a circular motion. Repeat at least 5 times in each direction.

Leg stretches
Start with the squat stand position. Move your weight back over one leg, straightening the other. Hold for about 5 seconds, and repeat with the weight over the other leg. Repeat 5 times.

Alternate toe touches
With both arms in the air, bring one arm down to touch the opposite toes, trying to get your forehead on the opposite knee, with the opposite hand still in the air. Repeat 5 times on both sides.

Bunny hops
With feet comfortably apart, bounce on your toes, getting your knees as close to your chest as possible with each hop. Repeat 5 times.

Warm-down

If play has been hard a warm-down afterwards will help the muscles remove waste deposits and prevent build-up of lactic acid which results in stiffness and swollen muscles after play. Competitive players find that warm-down results in a faster recovery between matches.

The knock-up

This is the final preparation for play and consists of hitting shots to your opponent without putting him or her under too much pressure. Remember the game hasn't started and there is no point in placing the shuttle out of reach. It should be a practice for both players and not just for one player to try out winning shots while the other merely picks the shuttle from the floor and feeds it back. A tracksuit should be worn throughout warm-up and knock-up as it prevents heat loss. Muscles only perform properly, without injury, when warm.

The grip

There is no grip suitable to play all strokes. In fact, there is a whole range of grips which allows you to perform the full repetoire of strokes. In order that you can change grip quickly and easily it is important that you hold the racket handle across the base of your fingers and not across the palm of your hand. In the performance of a stroke such as the round-the-head cross-court smash, the base of the handle could impare the movement of your wrist whereas it should be clear.

Achieving the grip

To achieve the basic grip from which all other grips can be found you should, if right handed, hold the racket by the shaft in your left hand with the racket head vertical. Your right palm is then placed gently against the handle with the fingers spread slightly apart. Close your fingers around the handle with only slight pressure. You can then rotate the handle using the thumb and forefingers to find all necessary grip variations. The basic difference between the backhand and forehand grips is that for the backhand the V between the thumb and forefinger is pointing slightly to the left of the racket head whereas for the forehand grip the V is pointing directly down the shaft to the edge of the racket head.

Loose and cocked wrists

Most elementary players, and indeed many professional players, use a *loose* wrist action to perform certain strokes when in fact they should be using a *cocked* wrist action. The loose wrist does not allow the player to impart any power into the shot. I explain this in more detail later in this chapter but in the meantime these illustrations show the basic difference.

Right: If you open your hand after finding your grip you will be able to see whether the handle is lying across your palm (wrong) (far right) or across the base of your fingers (correct) (right). Changing your grip is more difficult if the handle crosses the centre of your palm. The correct grip (right) will allow unrestricted movement and rotation of the wrist.

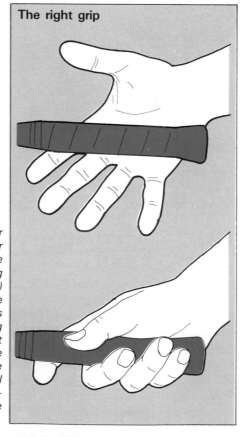

The right grip

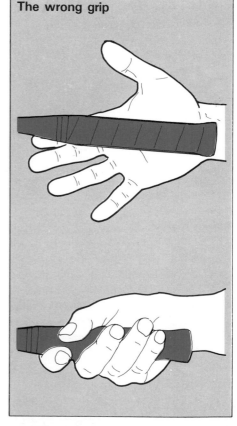

The wrong grip

Left: A good grip shows the forefinger spread slightly and the butt of the handle well clear of the wrist.

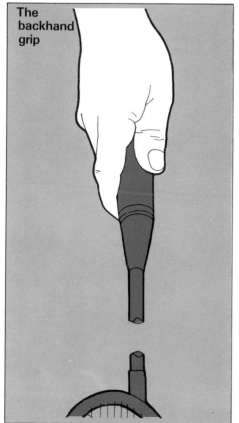

The backhand grip

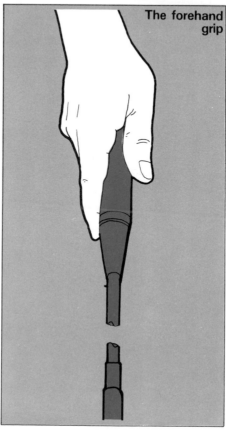

The forehand grip

Left: For the forehand grip the 'V' between thumb and forefinger points directly down to the head of the racket with no strings visible.

Far left: For the backhand grip the 'V' is pointing to an angled head with strings visible.

How to achieve the correct forehand grip

Hold the racket by the centre of the shaft with the fingers of the non-playing hand.

Place the palm of the playing hand flat against the string surface.

Slide the playing hand down the shaft of the racket until it makes contact with the handle.

Continue the movement of the playing hand until the heel of the palm touches the butt of the handle.

Gently close the fingers around the handle ensuring a degree of spread of the forefinger.

Far right: A whip action, used to impart power into a stroke.

Power-producing actions

In order to impart the maximum power into a stroke the wrist must first be *cocked* and the arm slightly bent at the elbow in preparation for the stroke. The hand uncocks throughout the stroke by a turning action of the wrist and forearm. Club players rarely cock their wrist sufficiently and consequently power is lost through a loose or weak wrist. There are three main actions: the tap, the push and the whip, although you may hear many other words used to describe the same actions.

The tap action

The power-producing action produced by uncocking your wrist is checked abruptly before the wrist is fully uncocked and simultaneously on impact with the shuttle. There is the sensation of a rebound of the hand as the movement is checked and a feeling of tremendous power on impact. The main strokes in which the tap action is used are the net kill and the backhand clear, but there are many others.

The whip action

Here the power-producing action remains unchecked and your hand uncocks on the completion of the stroke. With this complete follow-through you experience the sensation of your hand whipping in line with the acceleration of the racket head. It is possible to perform a slow whip, as certain forms of drop shot.

The push action

With your wrist cocked and elbow slightly bent as before, keep your wrist cocked throughout the stroke. An example of a stroke using the push action is the net block to the smash. The pushing action involves the straightening of the arm at the elbow, which offers great control over the pace of the shuttle and direction of flight.

Below: A cocked wrist with the hand almost at right angles to the forearm.

Bottom: A loose wrist with the hand and forearm in the same place.

Below right: With the powerful tap action the follow-through of the wrist is checked when the forearm and wrist are in line.

Cocked wrist and loose wrist

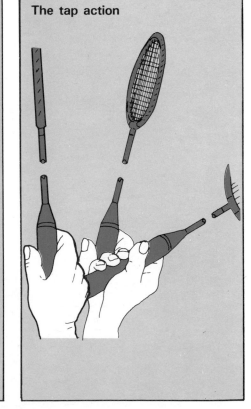

The tap action

Varying the racket face

In order to increase the effectiveness of your shots and the deceptive quality of your game, it is possible to change the direction of the shuttle by varying the angle of the face of your racket.

Square-on strokes

These strokes are played with the racket face square on (at right angles) to the flight path of the shuttle. The energy imparted to the shuttle is at its maximum as the force on impact is directly through the centre of the shuttle. The flat or power smash is the best example of a square-on stroke. Such a smash will land towards the back of the court.

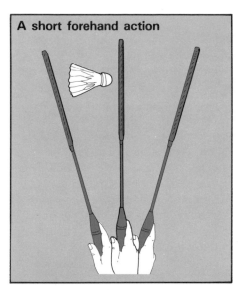

A short forehand action

Left: For a flat stroke, at the point of impact the shuttle is at right angles to the stringing surface and all energy is transmitted through the centre of the shuttle. The feathers do not brush against the strings as with slicing strokes.

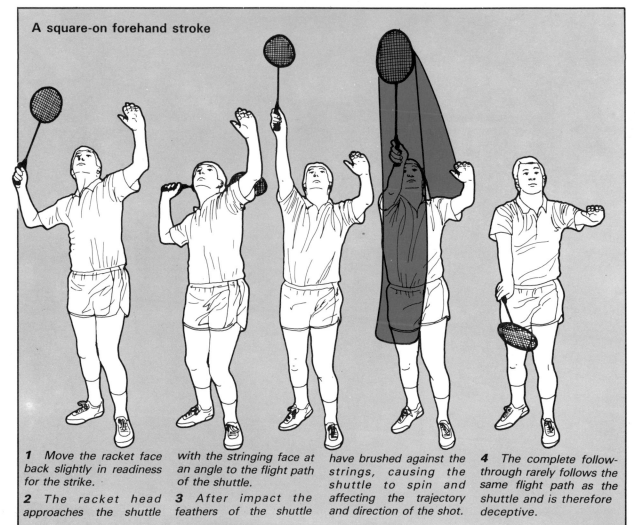

A square-on forehand stroke

1 Move the racket face back slightly in readiness for the strike.
2 The racket head approaches the shuttle with the stringing face at an angle to the flight path of the shuttle.
3 After impact the feathers of the shuttle have brushed against the strings, causing the shuttle to spin and affecting the trajectory and direction of the shot.
4 The complete follow-through rarely follows the same flight path as the shuttle and is therefore deceptive.

Slicing strokes

These strokes are played with the racket face at an angle to the flight path of the shuttle. The energy imparted to the shuttle is not at a maximum, but the slice action causes the shuttle to spin and the contact of the feathers on the strings of the racket head offers additional control to the player. The spinning of the shuttle also affects its flight path. In the case of the sliced smash, you would be able to bring the shuttle down far more steeply, and it would land one or two yards in front of the flat smash. If you slice the shuttle more severely with the same action the result would be a fast drop landing even closer to the net, around the front service line.

The slicing action

The sliced stroke

1 *Move the racket face back slightly in readiness for the strike.*
2 *The racket head approaches the shuttle with the stringing face at an angle to flight path of shuttle.*

3 *After impact the feathers of the shuttle have brushed against the strings, causing the shuttle to spin and affecting the trajectory and direction of the shot.*
4 *The complete follow-through rarely follows the same flight path as the shuttle and is consequently deceptive.*

The reverse sliced stroke

1 The preparation and movement of the racket hand back slightly in readiness for the strike is the same for all strokes.
2 The anti-clockwise movement of the wrist turns the racket face so that it is at an angle to the flight of the oncoming shuttle.
3/4 The shuttle is struck from the 'round the head' position.
5 The follow-through is away from the body.

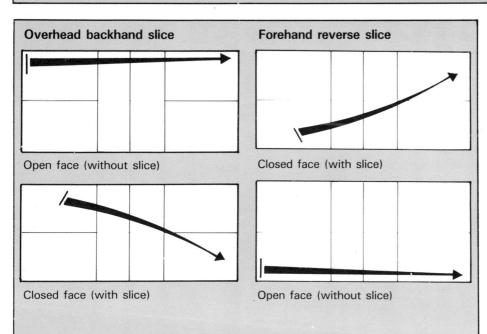

Overhead backhand slice

Open face (without slice)

Closed face (with slice)

Forehand reverse slice

Closed face (with slice)

Open face (without slice)

Above: This provides a cross-court alternative when taking a shuttle from the 'round the head' position.

Left: The north–south plane represents the directions of the follow through of the racket in all shots. From the forehand or backhand court the slicing action produces a cross-court alternative instead of a straight return down the side of the court. The trajectory becomes steeper the heavier the slice (the more oblique the face of the racket in relation to the shuttle on impact).

The service

The service begins each point and the player has the opportunity to place the shuttle carefully. There are a number of alternatives to choose from: the low serve, and deep serves which can be executed in different ways.

The rules of badminton state that the shuttle must be struck on its base, and that it must be below the server's waist when struck. The racket head must be below the server's hand at the moment of impact. This means that the shuttle will always rise upwards to travel over the net.

The low service

This is the staple diet of doubles play and indeed in the modern singles game the low service is frequently used by those players who like to commence a rally with a lift from their opponent.

The short service

The short service is executed from the corner of the court formed by the centre line and the front service line. The aim is to get the shuttle to pass as low as possible over the net, even 2" or 3" above the net, without risking hitting the net.

You should aim the shuttle somewhere along the front service line of the diagonally opposite service court. Were the receiver to allow your service to drop, it should fall behind the front service line.

The short service is performed with wrist cocked and a push action. While the area of court that the shuttle would land into on a high service is important, generally players are content to aim for a point midway along the rear service line. However, with the short service, variation of the point at which the shuttle passes over the net is very important.

The backhand short serve

The shuttle is held well in front of the body and is therefore closer to the net than with the forehand short serve.

This gives your opponent less time to consider a reply. The backhand grip is used with the thumb up the back of the racket for control and to help produce power if the flick action is needed. A short backswing is all that is necessary which gives the receiver little time to anticipate the serve. The elbow is high and there is little movement of the arm above this joint. It is particularly difficult to rush the backhand serve and because of this fact its popularity is on the increase. I also consider that it is an easy service to learn if taught correctly.

The forehand service

The artwork opposite shows the forehand flick (right) with the wrist releasing just prior to impact; and the forehand short service (far right) with the wrist remaining cocked.

1

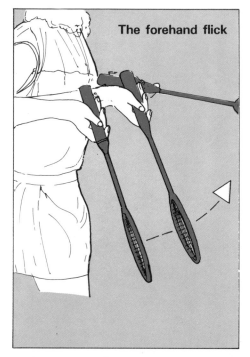

The forehand flick

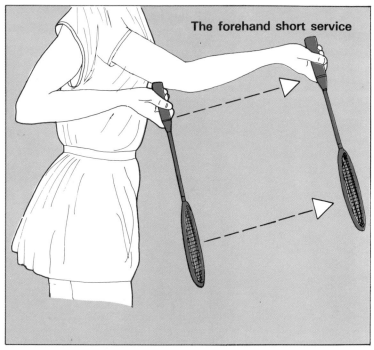

The forehand short service

The backhand service action

2

3

The racket is held well in front of the body ensuring that the position of the shuttle on the racket head is below the level of the waist.

A very short back swing is all that is required, which has the added benefit of disguise should a flick service be required.

A gentle lifting of the forearm from the elbow together with only a slight movement of the wrist produces a good low service.

The high service

This shot uses a whip action played with the racket face square on and is most commonly used in the singles game. It is important to hit the shuttle as high as possible so that it completes its trajectory on an almost vertical path. If allowed to drop it would land just inside the back line.

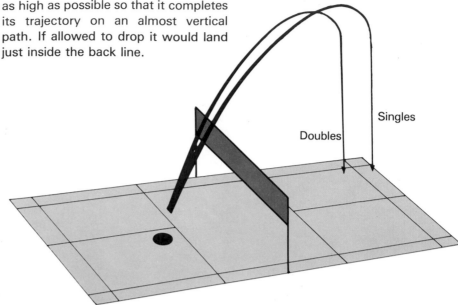

In the high service in doubles the shuttle lands vertically just in front of the doubles back service line.

In the high service in singles the shuttle lands vertically just inside the base line.

1 Prepare with racket held high and the shuttle held in front of the face.

2 The racket head is brought back and then as the racket commences its forward motion the shuttle is released.

3 The wrist uncocks upon follow through after impact. Do keep your eyes on the shuttle.

4 The racket and arm lift high in the air and the eyes move up to follow the flight path of the shuttle. The right leg pivots on the toes but the foot doesn't lift off the floor.

1

2

The deep high service

This is sometimes used in the doubles game, when the shuttle must land inside the second back line. The most common high service used is the flick, in which the server, with wrist cocked, follows the same preparatory movement as with the short service only to rapidly uncock the wrist just before impact. Such whipping action, if delivered properly, can be very deceptive as the receiver is also covering the low service.

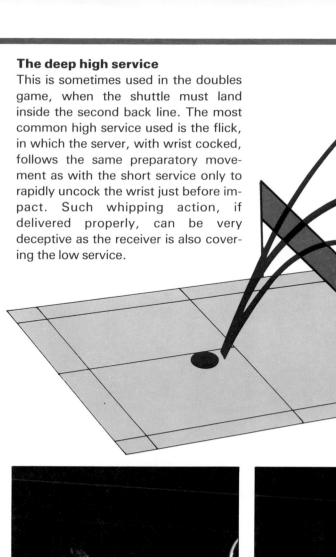
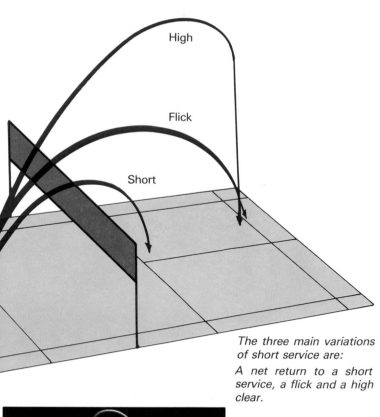

High

Flick

Short

The three main variations of short service are:

A net return to a short service, a flick and a high clear.

3

4

Return of service

Most players have a preference for the area of the court in which they like to receive service. For example some players prefer a short service directed to the centre of the court, particularly when they are in the right-hand court and they have developed an effective backhand return. On the other hand they may prefer a shuttle delivered to the centre of the service court. Generally it is quite difficult to make a positive return to a service delivered to the extreme edge of the court, although such a service is the most difficult to execute accurately. In the following diagram try to analyze which of the three you find the easiest or most difficult to receive.

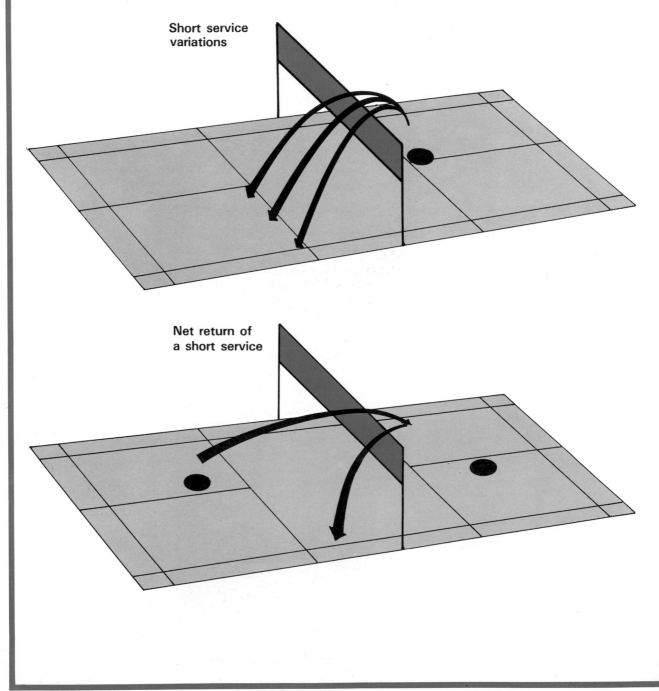

**Short service
variations**

**Net return of
a short service**

Effective return in singles

The principal service in the singles game is the high service to as near the baseline as possible. Such a service is difficult to smash to the floor and consequently the two principal replies are the clear and the drop. The clear return is either very high and frequently to the centre of the baseline or it follows a lower trajectory, the attacking clear, which is usually directed to either corner of the back court making an early interception as difficult as possible.

The drop return is either a slow drop or a sliced faster drop. The diagram shows the different flight paths of these two types of drop reply.

The slow drop is struck to fall as close to the net as possible so that the opponent has to move as far forward as possible to play the return. The sliced drop, which is usually struck more firmly, travels further back into court and is usually aimed towards the side of the singles court as far out of reach of the opponent as possible. The sliced drop is most effective in that it is very difficult for the opponent to play a tight net reply from a shuttle which falls so far into court. Because of the speed of the shot it is impossible for the opponent to get to the shuttle early enough to strike it close to the net.

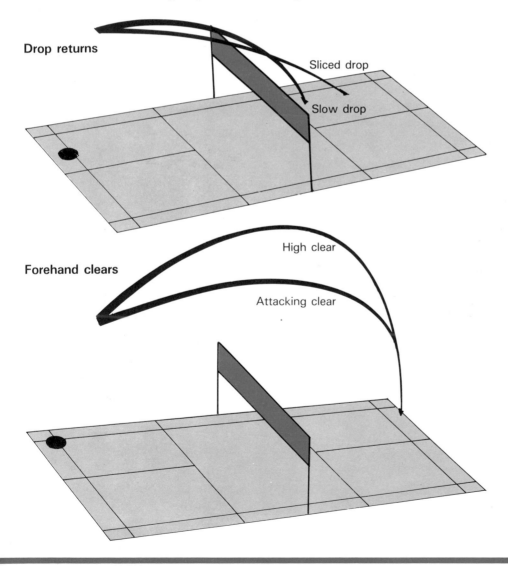

Drop returns

Sliced drop

Slow drop

Forehand clears

High clear

Attacking clear

Effective return in doubles

The principal service used in the doubles game is the short service. There are a number of ways of returning the various short services likely to be encountered. Firstly, there is the service to the centre of the court. When receiving you should stand with your leading foot close to the front service line. The exact position should allow you still to be able to get to the back of the court for a flick or high service. If the service is delivered more than a few inches above the net then the receiver should tap the shuttle downwards over the net either into an open area of court or safely down the centre of the court. The tap action will bring the shuttlecock sharply down to the floor. If the service passes close to the net then it will be difficult to hit the shuttlecock in a downwards direction but such a flight path is preferable if possible. Invariably the players who attack predominantly throughout the match win.

An excellent return to a tight short service is the brush return. A shuttle delivered to the centre of the court to a right-hander's backhand can be brushed down the centre of the court. Such a return is deceptive and therefore is difficult to return past the receiver to the back of the court or indeed tightly over the net. The illustration sequence shows the brushing action and the flight of the return. The two forecourt areas down each of the sidelines are also useful target areas for the receiver's return. These

Below: A good stance to receive service. The body is balanced and able to move forwards or backwards easily. The leading leg is close to the front service line and the racket is held in a position to cover all possible services.

A return to the forecourt sidelines

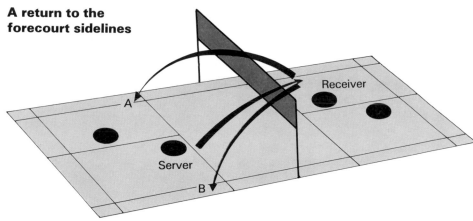

Left: A and B show the target areas of the court for the half court push.

areas are out of reach of the net player and are also difficult to cover by the player at the back of the court.

If the short service is really accurate and literally clips the top of the tape as it passes over the net then the receiver has two choices, either to play a net return or to lift the shuttle to the rear of the court. The net shot is played with a push action and the rear court lift is played with a whip action. It is important to take the shuttle as early as possible, particularly in the case of the net reply where the receiver wishes to give the server insufficient time to tap

the shuttle downwards from the top of the tape.

If the server in doubles flicks or delivers a high service then the receiver should move back as quickly as possible, get behind the shuttle and smash it to the floor. A smash down the side of the court is the most difficult for the receiver to cover although a smash down the centre of the court can also be difficult to return. The angle of return from a smash down the centre of the court is less and can be more easily cut off by the player waiting at the net.

Below: The sequence shows the racket head movement resulting from the turning action of the forearm and wrist.

The brushed net return

The backhand action

Most club level players have problems playing a good backhand. The reason is that they have never mastered the basic backhand action. Earlier I explained the power-producing action of the cocked wrist. To perform a good backhand this action is particularly important. It is a common mistake to try and play the backhand with a loose wrist — always cock your wrist.

Your thumb should be located up the side or back of the handle, depending on whether the shuttle is struck behind or in front of the body. The thumb provides the surge of power necessary to produce the correct tap action. The position of the thumb varies in order not to restrict the movement of the wrist as it uncocks in line with the turning of the forearm. There is little movement of the shoulder which moves gently in the direction of the shuttle throughout the stroke. The artwork sequence below shows the racket and arm movement for a backhand clear.

It is important that the stroke cycle is completed in a smooth fluent fashion, with ease and economy, rather than with a jerky movement using excessive energy. Once a smooth action has been grooved into your play, perfect timing will produce the best results rather than exertion. Note that the point of impact is in line with the body. The shuttle can be struck from behind or in front of the body but there is a loss of power if struck from behind.

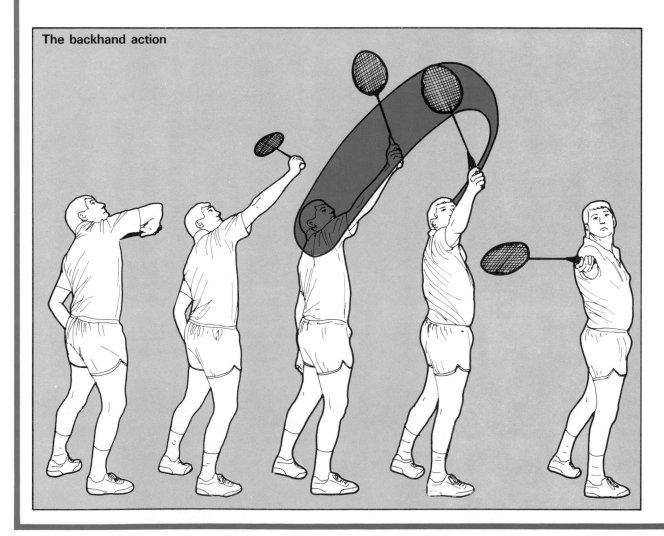

The backhand action

Backhand smash

The action is the same as for the backhand clear except that the wrist has a less restricted turn or follow through which produces the downward trajectory from impact. The basic action used is the tap action. The photographic sequence shows the racket and arm movement for the backhand smash.

The point of impact is fractionally in front of the body line perhaps 10-15cm/ 4-6" in front of the impact point for the backhand clear. It is important that the wrist remains quite firm throughout the stroke, particularly on impact, although there is a greater turning of the forearm than with the clear.

The popular trajectory for the backhand smash.

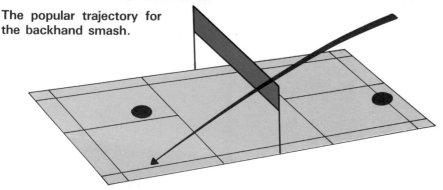

Backhand drop

Here the whip action allows for a greater follow through of the wrist. The action is very relaxed and a slow drop landing close to the net is the result. The sequence shows the racket and arm movement for the backhand slow drop.

The first picture demonstrates the position of readiness with elbow bent and wrist cocked. The second shows the moment of impact at a point when the shuttle is level with the player's head. In the last photograph the wrist follows through completely after impact in the direction of the flight of the shuttle.

Brushed backhand drop

By rolling the wrist the brushed backhand drop can be played. This shot is particularly deceptive and the shuttle flies close to the net as a result of the brushing action. The sequence shows the racket and arm movements for the straight brushed drop.

The point of impact is similar to the normal backhand drop but a more severe turning of the forearm and wrist is necessary, with a follow-through down a path in front of the body. The wrist uncocks completely upon follow-through.

Cross-court sliced drop

By rolling the wrist in a clockwise direction the cross-court sliced drop can be struck. Slicing the shuttle allows the player to play the drop very tight over the net if so desired. The sequence shows the racket and arm movement for the cross-court drop.

The position of readiness and point of impact remain as for other forms of backhand drop. However, the wrist remains cocked throughout the stroke and the follow-through is across and then away from the player's body.

Backhand drive

If a whip action is used an emphatic swing of the arm and a complete follow-through of the wrist takes place. Unlike the relaxed movement of the backhand drop the movement of the wrist is much faster resulting in a much greater speed of shuttle.

If a tap action is used the wrist follow-through is checked. Generally this action is used when the player is close to the net. The arm and racket follow a

Sara Sankey lunging sideways to deliver a backhand drive straight down the line.

path line at approximately waist height and parallel to the floor. The stroke can be performed either straight down the side of the court or alternatively cross-court. Whilst the shuttle is usually struck with a square-on racket face it is possible to slice or undercut the shuttle to take pace off the stroke. This slicing action also affects the trajectory of the shuttle and can often provide the player with more control when returns just above net-tape height are required.

Backhand defence

A downwards flight path to the backhand can be dealt with in a number of ways depending on the pace and type of shot delivered by the opponent. Nevertheless basic principles apply to all returns. Use the backhand grip, as described on page 49. Secondly, and most importantly, the racket should be held well out in front of the body. This allows the shuttle to be struck earlier, and allows for a greater variation of the angle of return. One variation of particular importance is the flat return which must be struck before the shuttlecock drops too low. In this form of defence the opponent is forced to either lift the shuttle or at best reply with another flat trajectory shot.

The variations possible within the bounds of these basic principles depend upon whether the return is performed with a flat racket face or an angled racket face. Using the whip action the shuttle can be returned high to the rear of the court and by using the push action a block to the net can be performed. The net block is a very effective return of the smash as it puts your opponent on the defence. It is important that while your wrist remains cocked your arm is relaxed as your elbow straightens.

The backhand block return

Preparing to receive the smash with the racket held across and in front of the body.

Wrist cocked and elbow slightly bent on impact.

Wrist remains cocked, the arm lifts and the elbow straightens to complete the stroke.

The forehand action

A short forehand action showing the turning of the forearm and wrist similar in action to throwing a ball.

The wrist is cocked at the starting position. As your wrist follows through so does your shoulder and upper arm move in the direction of the shot and most importantly your forearm turns. The photographic sequence shows the racket and arm movement for the forehand action.

The forehand clear
The racket in the starting position is pointing towards the oncoming shuttle. As the shuttle approaches the point of impact your wrist fully cocks and your arm and shoulder are pulled back in readiness for the strike. Your whole body commences the turning

The racket moves back before commencing its forward motion. A total follow through completes the stroke.

movement and in doing so your shoulder and forearm move forward, and the turning of your forearm and unleashing of your cocked wrist complete the sequence to the point of impact. Your arm and racket follow through with the racket movement being checked so that you can resume the position of readiness for the next shot as quickly as possible.

This forehand action is very much a throwing action and the movements are similar to throwing a stone high into the air. Extra power can be achieved by bending the torso at the waist as this adds bodyweight to the shot. A strong, flexible back is therefore a very important asset. The high clear is played with the whip action whereas the punchy attacking clear is played with a tap action, in which the wrist remains cocked.

The diagram on page 61 shows the difference in trajectory for the high clear and the attacking clear.

The forehand smash

The tap action used in the attacking clear is also used in the smash. The basic difference between the strokes is that the point of impact of the smash is just in front of your body and your wrist has released further at the point of impact.

Many players gain power by jumping off the ground just before playing the stroke. It is important when doing so that your body should be moving in a downward direction at the point of impact, otherwise you would lose power as opposed to gaining it. It is of no real advantage, other than for a steeper angle of smash, to jump high off the ground. A few inches is sufficient providing your sense of timing is accurate enough and your body is moving down to the ground at the time of impact. Indeed it is ideal if at the strike your feet are just starting to re-make contact with the floor as this enables you to achieve balance quickly for the next shot. In the following sequence look closely at the position of the feet during the various stages of the stroke.

Bending at the waist can also add power to the smash. With this bending movement, the upper body moves for-

Right: A jump smash performed square-on to the net with the feet only slightly apart. The extra power comes from the straightening of the trunk and the downwards motion of the body.

1 The use of a skip foot action to lift off the ground.

2 The racket moves back as the feet leave the floor.

3 The impact takes place just as the bodyweight commences its downwards movement and the follow-through is completed as the feet regain contact with the floor.

4 The body is in balance on completion of the stroke.

ward and adds weight to the shot. The difficulty is in co-ordinating arm and body action with the jump into a smooth harmonious stroke. However, practice makes perfect.

A typical trajectory for the forehand smash.

The steeper trajectory is possible with the use of a jump movement on a smash.

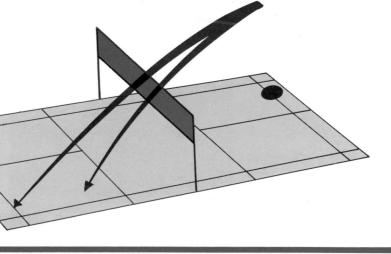

The forehand drop

The build up to this shot should be the same as for the forehand clear and for the smash, except that when the racket head approaches the point of impact the movement is checked and the follow through becomes slow, deliberate and controlled. If you hit the shuttle with a flat racket then the checking action needs to be very pronounced as a relatively slow follow-through will be required to produce a drop which passes just over the net.

The sliced drop

This shot needs greater racket-head speed. It is done by only slightly checking the speed of follow-through. It is a very deceptive shot, therefore, as it is most difficult to tell it apart from a smash until the shuttle actually comes off the racket head.

The slice can be achieved in two ways. For the normal sliced drop the wrist turns in a clockwise direction and a chopping action is needed with the racket face at an angle to the intended direction of the shuttle. The photographic sequence shows this arm and racket action.

The stroke is extremely deceptive. Opponents find it very difficult to anticipate the pace of the shuttle or indeed its direction, for the shuttle will not travel in the same direction as the racket as it follows through. Indeed, for such a glancing blow, the severity of slice can vary greatly, and it can be fun to experiment with the angle of the racket face in practice. This stroke is commonly used from the forehand court across to the opponents' forehand.

1

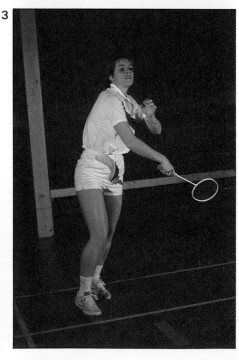

1 *Preparing for the stroke.*
2 *Striking the shuttle with an oblique racket face.*
3 *A complete follow through across the player's body.*

1

2

1 Preparing for the stroke with racket head back.
2 Striking the shuttle 'round the head' rolling the wrist in an anticlockwise direction.
3 A follow through away from the body as the wrist fully uncocks.

3

The reverse sliced drop

A more difficult shot to perform this involves rolling the wrist in a more unnatural anti-clockwise direction. The sequence shows the arm and racket movement involved.

This shot can be very effective from the backhand court if you want to use a forehand stroke. Such a 'round-the-head' shot is very effective and it is worth noting that a 'frying pan' grip (shown below) will help to allow the full movement of the wrist necessary to perform the stroke properly.

Similar fast slicing actions can be used with smashes and clears. You will be amazed at the variations in speed and direction made possible by slicing the shuttle.

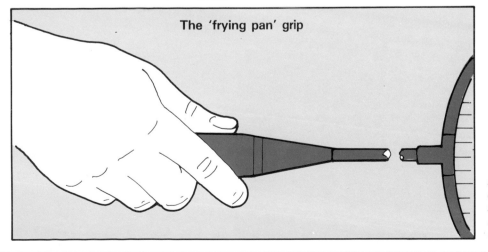

The 'frying pan' grip

Left: The 'frying pan' grip can be useful in striking shuttles 'round the head' as it allows full movement of the wrist.

The forehand drive

The forehand drive is the term used to describe the stroke that is played hard and flat, that results in the shuttle flying only a few inches above the height of the net. In general the shuttle should be struck in front of your body and directed straight down the side of the court or, alternatively, across court. The cross-court forehand drive can be very deceptive when played slightly behind your body but this is a difficult stroke to perform and demands a very strong wrist. It is usually better to try and take the shuttle as early as possible and by doing so strike the shuttle as far out in front of the body as possible.

1

2

1 Position of readiness as for backhand defence.

2 Racket moves across body to cover forehand.

3 Knees slightly bent and wrist cocked. A forward push of the shoulder and arm is all that is required.

This sequence is for the block defence with complete opening of the cocked wrist for a high defence to the rear of the court — a whip action.

3

The forehand defence

Generally speaking players find it more difficult to defend on the forehand than on the backhand. This is possibly because it does not always feel natural to hold the racket out in front of your body. If you do not do this then you will not have time to change to a forehand grip if a smash is directed to the forehand side when you are defending with a backhand stance. Otherwise the same principles as for the backhand defence apply. The sequence shows a well-produced forehand defensive stroke.

Below: The push defence can land in any selected position from the area of the block defence to the rear of the court.

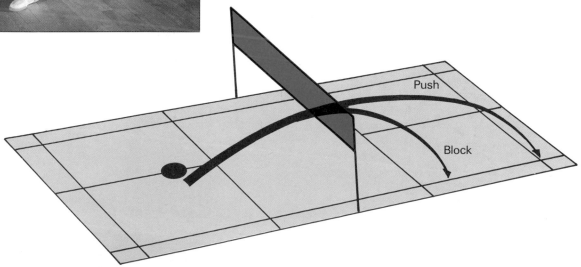

The net shots

The net shot

The action used here is the push. The wrist remains cocked so that control of the shuttle is maximized. The elbow comes back in preparation for the stroke and the shot is delivered as the elbow joint straightens with the wrist remaining firm.

Ideally the shuttle should be taken as close to the top of the net as possible and this is achieved by straightening your arm with your hand pointing upwards at an angle of about 45°.

The photographic sequence shows that the net shot is performed with a lunge movement with racket hand and arm, but in front of the body. The wrist remains cocked and the forward movement of the arm provides the energy for the stroke. Take the shuttle as early as possible.

The spin net shot

The slicing action used here causes the shuttle to spin making it more difficult for your opponent to control the return. It is achieved by the racket face meeting the shuttle at an angle so that the force applied to the shuttle is to one side of its centre. The result is the shuttle rotates or spins around a central axis.

By changing the direction of the movement of the racket head from downwards to upwards you will cause the shuttle to tumble as well as spin.

This may appear quite difficult to achieve but if you experiment with a number of variations of glancing blows to the shuttle you will be surprised at some of the effective shots that result.

You will see from the photographic sequence that the wrist is uncocked throughout the stroke.

Return of the net shot

The basic net shot can be returned in four main ways.

● If the net shot is not a good one then the shuttle should be merely tapped to the floor.

● If the shuttle is loose, but not loose enough for a simple tap kill, then a brush reply can be made, hitting the shuttle to the forecourt just past the short service line, down the centre of the court or to the sides. This stroke is another example of the slice action whereby the racket face is at an angle to the intended flight path of the shuttle.

● If the net shot is tight over the net then another net shot in reply is a good choice. If the shuttle is taken early then the opponent will be forced to lift the shuttle in one way or another. This will allow you to attack the shuttle forcing your opponent to lift yet again. A player who attacks throughout the majority of a match invariably wins.

● If your opponent's net shot is tight and he is directly covering a possible net reply then the best return is an underhand clear or lift to the back of the court. The action here is similar to the high service or, if a lower trajectory is required, the flick service.

Return of the spin net shot

Again the same four types of return are possible but only the tap and brush return are played in the same way.

The net reply and the underarm lift must be played with a sliced action. Such an action counters the spin on the shuttle, to a lesser extent, but in much the same way as in table tennis.

The net reply is played in the same manner as the spin net shot.

The underarm lift is played in this situation with the racket head following a curved path.

Right: Moreton Frost of Denmark performing a spin net shot.

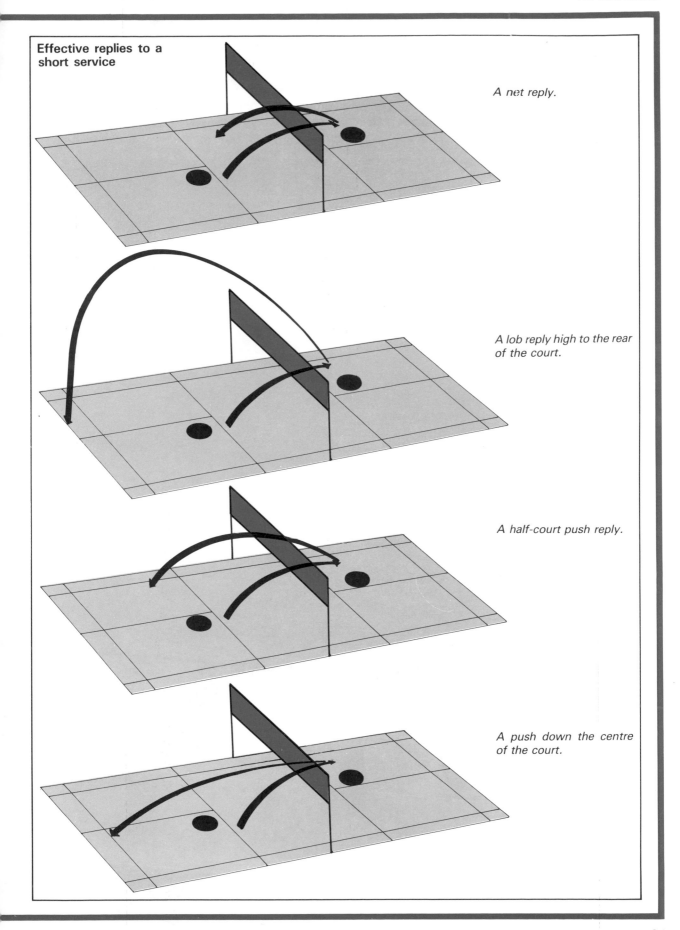

Effective replies to a
short service

A net reply.

*A lob reply high to the rear
of the court.*

A half-court push reply.

*A push down the centre
of the court.*

Practices for stroke skills

If you are a member of a club where individual practice is not readily possible the following skill routines can probably be practised in a normal club night. Others can be practised with a partner on a vacant court. It is fair to say, however, that all the practices are fun and should be enjoyed.

1 *Hitting the shuttle on the rebound against a wall.*

2 *Forehand and backhand: hitting the shuttle into the air.*

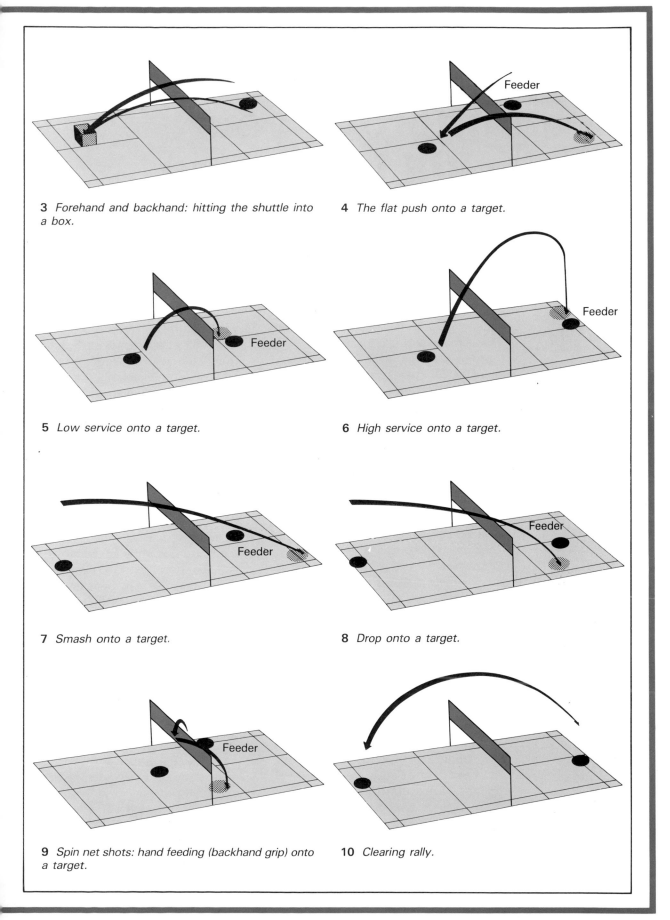

3 *Forehand and backhand: hitting the shuttle into a box.*

4 *The flat push onto a target.*

5 *Low service onto a target.*

6 *High service onto a target.*

7 *Smash onto a target.*

8 *Drop onto a target.*

9 *Spin net shots: hand feeding (backhand grip) onto a target.*

10 *Clearing rally.*

Chapter 5 Improve your skill in moving

by Jake Downey

Badminton is a game which appeals to many players and spectators for the movement that takes place. No other game contains such a range and variety of movement nor places so many different demands on the athletic/gymnastic potential of the players. Only gymnasts and dancers require more general body skill than the badminton player who in addition must possess the explosive movement of the athlete combined with the hitting skills of the martial arts and the control and grace of a dancer. It is the game of all games for the expression of beauty, speed, power and control in movement.

For these reasons the players' skills in moving on the court become as important as their skill in hitting the shuttle. It is often the lack of skill in moving and the consequent inability to get into an effective hitting position which causes errors to occur in the execution of a stroke. And yet this very important aspect of the game is either neglected or limited to a few comments about the need for good footwork and balance without any account of what these are or how they can be developed.

All players can develop their natural skill in moving providing that they spend some time practising some basic movement components which are common to many sports in general and badminton in particular. The extent to which they can do so is determined by players' natural ability and the extent to which they are prepared to practise.

There are several ways in which players develop their skill in moving. Many do so naturally during their childhood in street and school playground games, eg such dodging and chasing games as 'tickey', 'he', 'tag'; climbing and swinging; relay races; skipping and jumping games, roller skating, skateboarding, cycling, and ball games.

Many people develop movement skills during the usual school physical education programme in which they experience moving in a number of specific activities; gymnastics, ball games, swimming, athletics and dance. If you have experienced many of these activities then you will already have developed a certain degree of skill in moving which will serve you well on the badminton court.

If however you consider yourself a poor mover, regardless of whether you have or have not experienced these activities, then there is a third way to develop your skill in moving. You can practise specific movement skills in your learning of badminton. Before I explain what these are just reflect for a while and imagine that you are watching a game of badminton. Focus your attention on one player moving about the court.

What will you see in your mind's

eye? You will see the player performing a whole range of actions and patterns of movement as he or she travels from one place to another in the court to hit the shuttle. All this movement can be analyzed in terms of six basic components which players need to practise in order to develop their skill in moving. These are: posture and balance, starting and stopping, step patterns, transitions (changes of direction), lunges, jumping and landing. Of these, posture and balance are common to them all. Each component can be developed separately although they are all inter-related. Try to imagine the player performing these.

The benefits of analyzing the movement in this way is that it will enable you to identify your movement needs and to have some specific aspect of your movement to practise. You will be able to improve your body skill (skill in moving) just as you can practise your racket skill (skill in hitting the shuttle).

I will now explain each one in more detail and also provide some awareness exercises and on- and off-court development practices. First, however, a warning about safety.

Above: Lunges, jumping and landing are all essential movements that you need to develop and practise. You can perform specific exercises to improve these body skills and play better badminton.

The movement components

1   Posture and balance

Your body occupies space (body space), is surrounded by space and is subject to the force of gravity.

Posture Good posture is when you have an awareness and control of the positions of your body parts in relation to your body space to the extent that you feel *centred,* symmetrically balanced within yourself.

Balance Good balance requires an awareness and control of the positions of your body parts in relation to gravity. You should feel *centred,* in balance, in relation to the ground.

Awareness exercises
1   Posture

Stand tall as if stretched upwards in your back and at the rear of your head. Your shoulders should be relaxed and stomach muscles lightly tensed and pulled in until you feel that each part of your body from the head downwards is resting directly on the part below. This is the position for good posture. Now try the following awareness exercises which will help you to identify when you are centred and not centred.

a   Centring the head

Tilt your head forwards — return to centre.

Tilt your head backwards — return to centre.

Tilt your head sideways — return to centre.

Centring the head

Safety

1   Footwear: ensure that your badminton shoes enable you to get a good grip on the floor surface and are well cushioned to absorb the force of your contact with the ground (see page 11).

2   Knees: it is important in all exercises that involve rapid and sometimes excessive knee bending that care is taken to ensure that the knee bends in the correct alignment. The knee is a hinge type joint and consequently any twisting movements or any uneven bending of the knee may cause strain and possible injury.

The general rule is to make sure that the centre of the knee passes directly over the centre of the foot. I would recommend that you look to make sure that you bend your knees in the correct alignment.

3   Warm-up and warm-down: walk around or jog (on the spot) and do some stretching/loosening exercises (see page 30) before you begin movement practices. This will help you to perform quality work and reduce the risk of injury. After practising, depending on how vigorously you have worked, warm-down by walking around and some loosening exercises.

Centring the shoulders

b Centring the shoulders
Raise both shoulders — lower the shoulders
Raise the right shoulder and lower it and repeat with the left shoulder.
Pull the shoulders forwards and backwards — return to centre.

c Centring the trunk
Stand tall with head and shoulders centred. Let your trunk collapse forwards and return to centre. Let your trunk collapse backwards and return to centre.

d Walk and/or run with good posture.

2 Balance
a Swaying
Stand centred with feet together. Sway forwards and return to centre, backwards and then centre and sideways and centre. You should feel the toes, big toe especially, gripping the ground to maintain balance. Do this with eyes closed to heighten the awareness.

b Travelling
Travel around while walking, running, skipping, side stepping, jumping. Stop quickly and centre your body in balance. Do not look at the ground when stopping — keep the head level and eyes looking forwards.

Centring the trunk

Talbot's tips

The key to good movement is *balance*. If you are not balanced when playing a stroke then your recovery will be slow. The calf and quadricept muscles play an important role in controlling balance, particularly in the production of the important lunge movement. Calf raises and half squats will help to tone the important muscle groups for better balanced movement around the court.

Opposite: You need to develop not only your technique but also your movement skills in order to play badminton well. A wide range of patterns of action and movement is essential as you move around the court to hit the shuttle.

3 Starting and stopping

The ability to accelerate from a stationary position and then stop quickly is an integral part of the game. Examples of starting are when receiving serve, and when in mid-court defence. Examples of stopping are when running fowards to play a net shot, or when running backwards to stop in a position to smash.

Awareness exercises
Starting

The ability to start quickly depends on technique, balance and posture, flexibility and strong leg muscles. Before you can move away from the spot you will have to transfer your body weight into the direction you wish to travel with your feet then ready to thrust you in the new direction. There are several ways of doing this.

1 Stand upright in balance with your knees slightly bent and your weight on the balls of your feet. Now sway slightly forwards to transfer your weight towards the direction you want to go. Push down with your feet and extend your legs rapidly to thrust you away from the spot. Do this slowly to get the feel of the movement and then quickly until you accelerate away from the spot.

2 The most effective way to accelerate from the spot is to use a bounce or jump start. This type of start, which causes the thigh and calf muscles to extend with eccentric contraction (extend quickly whilst under tension), makes use of the stretch reflex in these muscles and has the effect of 'charging' them which enables them to exert more force when contracting during the push off from the spot.

A small jump as you bounce your knees enables you to transfer your body weight ready to travel in a particular direction.

3 Try the above exercises with your feet apart positioned side by side and with one foot in front of the other. Practise travelling in different directions, eg forwards, backwards and sideways.

Stopping

To stop still in balance whilst travelling at speed you will have to transfer your body weight quickly to the opposite direction. If you are travelling forwards your body weight will be more in front so you will simply transfer it backwards by bringing your feet and legs towards the front. In doing so you will experience the sensation of 'holding back' your body in the opposite direction to that which you are travelling.

Practise this by sprinting in a direction and then stop quickly in balance and in stillness.

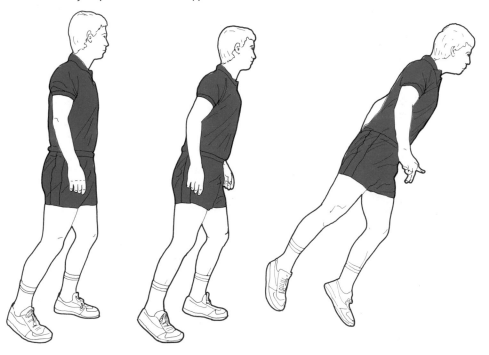

Right: This sequence of awareness exercises demonstrates one method of starting quickly. With knees slightly bent and weight on balls of feet, stand upright, and then sway slightly forwards to transfer weight in desired direction. Now push down and extend legs quickly to thrust you away.

4 Travelling

This is the aspect of movement which we usually refer to as 'footwork' when you walk, run, side step and chasse. Whatever means are used it is most important that you travel with quality of movement, ie fluently, smoothly and softly. For this reason you should practise various step patterns in shadow badminton sequences and do so without making a sound, as if with 'soft feet'.

5 Transitions

This term refers to the ability to change direction quickly and smoothly, ie going from side to side or forwards and backwards. It involves good posture and balance with the ability stop quickly to transfer the body weight into a new direction and start off again in that direction in one fluent movement.

Awareness exercises

Travel at various speeds and perform quick sharp changes of direction. Concentrate on the transitions and practise until you can perform them quickly and smoothly:

a   from forwards to backwards
b   from backwards to forwards
c   from side to side
d   on zig-zag pathways

6 Lunge and recovery

A lunge is simply a large extending

Below: You can practise awareness exercises to develop your ability to lunge and recover in badminton. Good posture and balance, especially in the half lunge, are essential.

step onto a flexing racket leg* which is performed in various directions in the court. The ability to lunge and recover is an essential part of badminton.

*Note: the racket leg or foot relates to the racket hand. It is the right foot for right-handed players and the left foot for left-handed players.

There is the full lunge used when a player is late getting to the shuttle and has to perform an extra stretch to hit it, and the half lunge, a partially extended step, performed when the player has time to get into a more comfortable hitting position. The half lunge will allow you to maintain good posture and balance while hitting the shuttle and also enable you to recover more easily and with less effort.

From the outstretched lunge position there are several ways to perform the recovery and centre your body ready to move away from the spot.

First, you can transfer your body weight by swaying backwards onto the rear foot, flexing the rear knee while doing so and bringing the racket foot closer to the rear foot.

Second, you can move the rear foot

Below: This sequence shows the series of positions in the lunge, starting with the attack position and then pushing off with your rear foot to lunge forwards onto your right to hit the shuttle.

The lunge

towards the flexed racket leg, flexing the knee of the rear leg as you do so. This can be done after the hit or whilst you are performing the hit.

The result of either action is that you will be centred with both legs flexed ready to travel quickly away from the spot.

Awareness exercises

1 Performing the lunge from a stationary position. Stand centred with knees flexed and feet shoulder width apart. These exercises can be performed at home.

a Lunge forwards to the right forecourt and recover; the left forecourt and recover.

b Lunge sideways to the right mid-court and recover; the left mid-court and recover.

c Lunge backwards to the right rear court and recover; the left rear court and recover.

Note: Practise both types of recovery.

2 Practise the lunge while travelling at speed. When travelling at speed you will use the non-racket leg to make a preparatory slowing down movement immediately prior to lunging on the racket foot. This is done by turning the non-racket foot outwards at a 45° angle and flexing the knee to lower the centre of gravity, to check the speed and to prepare for the thrust forwards onto the racket foot. The non-racket

foot can be turned outwards to the side of the racket foot, directly behind it or crossed over behind the racket foot.

Jumping and landing

This movement component is a very dynamic aspect of the game and as such good technique is essential in performing the various jumps and landings that take place. Once you have grasped the basic techniques of jumping and landing, can control the flight through the air, and have developed an awareness for good posture and balance, then jumping and landing backwards in the rear court, sideways in the mid-court and forwards in the forecourt will be easily performed.

Jumping and landing is an athletic/gymnastic type event which, from a starting position in the court, comprises the approach run, the take-off, the flight, and the landing. In badminton two other factors must be included. First there is the stroke performed during the flight phase and then the recovery as the player travels into position to cover the probable replies.

Jumping

Although badminton jumps are given specific names, eg *diagonal jump* to the forehand rear court, there are only five basic jumps which you will have to learn in order to perform any type of badminton jump. The five basic jumps are:

1 from one foot to the same foot,
2 from one foot to the other foot,
3 from one foot to two feet,
4 from two feet to two feet,
5 from two feet to one foot.

These jumps will be performed when jumping for distance and/or height.

Examples of these with reference to badminton jumps are:

1 diagonal jump smash to the forehand rear court (one foot to two feet),

2 scissor jump smash to the backhand rear court (one foot to the other foot),

3 vertical jump smash (two feet to two feet),

Below: Landing lightly after a jump smash and making a quick recovery is a skill that even some top players find difficult. In order to land properly, you need to experiment jumping different heights and distances, always ensuring that you land lightly and retain your good posture.

4 side jump smash in the mid-court (one foot to two feet or two feet to two feet),
5 forward jump to the forecourt (one foot to the other foot or one foot to the same foot).

Awareness practices
Experiment using the five basic jumps and then work out which sort of basic jump you will use when performing the specific badminton jumps.

Landing
Many players at all levels fail to recover into position quickly after performing a jump smash because they lack skill in landing. The main task is to land lightly, complete the landing and then recover quickly ready to cover the probable replies. You will only do this if you know how to land properly.

There are three types of landing used after performing a jump:
1 the landing after a high jump in which you will approach the ground on a vertical flight path is usually performed with a deep landing as the legs contract to absorb the force of the landing, eg after a diagonal or vertical jump smash;
2 the landing after a distance jump in which you will travel on a horizontal flight path is usually performed with additional steps on landing to allow the flow of movement to continue with a gradual deceleration, eg after a scissor jump smash perfomed after a flick serve;
3 the landing after a jump whose flight path is a combination of vertical and horizontal travel is usually performed with an upward rebound jump on the spot to prevent further travel, eg after a forward jump into the forecourt to make a kill at the net.

In all jumping and landing good posture, balance and lightness in landing are important. After landing a transition is necessary to recover into position in the court.

Awareness practices
1 Experiment jumping for height and/or distance and practise the different sorts of landings. Make sure that you land lightly in balance with good posture.
2 Repeat **1** above but then, after completing the landing, perform a transition in order to recover into a new court position.

General practices for body skill
Below are some simple practices which will help you to develop more awareness in using your body and improve your skill in moving. In each of the following practices you should play a game of shadow badminton at medium pace with the emphasis on each movement component. Practise each exercise for 30-60 seconds according of how fit you are. Allow an equal number of seconds as a rest period between practices.
1 Posture and balance: play an imaginary game while keeping your back straight and head looking forwards.
2 Travelling: play without making a sound — as if with 'soft feet'.
3 Starting and stopping: play and emphasize the quickness of a controlled stop before performing a stroke, and a rapid acceleration in starting from the spot.
4 Transitions: play and show clearly quick, controlled changes in direction.
5 Lunge and recovery: play with the emphasis on half lunges and full lunges. Show clearly the preparatory slowing down movement in the lunge and the methods of recovery.
6 Jumping and landing: play and show clearly the different sorts of badminton jumps with emphasis on the related types of landings. Make sure that you land lightly and complete the landing fully before recovering into a new court position.

If you place as much emphasis on the practice of the movement components as you do on the practice of the strokes then you will develop your body skill as much as your racket skill.

Chapter 6 **Tactics**

The singles game

There are a number of basic principles to learn in order to be successful as a singles player.

Creating gaps

Perhaps the most fundamental tactic of the singles game is to move your opponent away from the centre of the court thereby creating gaps which are difficult to cover. The centre of the court is the area which the singles player establishes as a base from which to cover all shots. You must try to get back to base after playing a stroke as failure to do so effectively creates a gap which provides a target area for your opponent. Speed and movement play an important role in getting back to base and these factors are covered in more detail in Chapter 5. Therefore, the four main target areas in moving a player from base are the four corners of the court. These positions are shown in the diagram. Shots played to the centre net and centre base line are also effective in creating gaps.

Exploiting bad movement

This tactic can take a number of forms. A simple example is to create a gap which your opponent, through bad movement, finds it difficult to cover. A more subtle ploy is to play the shuttle back where it came from for an oppo-

Far left: movement characteristics can be analyzed and then exploited as a useful basic tactic particularly in the singles game.

Safety play

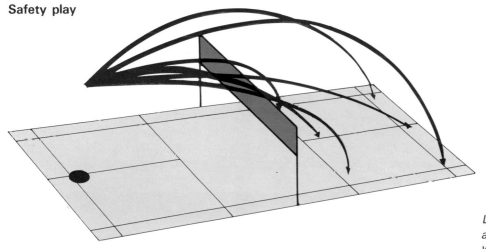

Left: the safety target areas are comfortably within the boundaries of the court.

Attacking the backhand

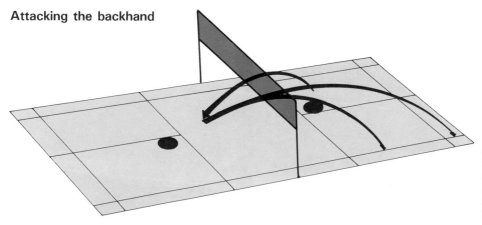

Left: attacking the backhand can often best be achieved by opening up the court with a drop to the opponent's forehand.

nent who, because of bad movement back to base, finds it difficult to turn and assume the same position adopted to play the previous shot. It is important in knocking up or in the early stages of a match to watch your opponent's movement to all four corners of the court. Invariably it will be apparent that movement to one or more of the corners is particularly bad. If so these corners should become regular target areas during the rallies. Players who do not have very good quadriceps (thigh muscles) have difficulty moving forwards to cover the net as they are unable to lunge properly.

These players compensate by taking the strain through keeping their legs close together which means they need to take extra steps and this slows them down. It is important to assess and exploit your opponent's movement imperfections as an important basic tactic.

Attacking the backhand

Many readers of this book will be of club level, and for those of you in this category the simple ploy of attacking an opponent's backhand is a most important tactic, for two reasons. Firstly, most players find it difficult to hit a good length clear off the backhand and secondly backhand strokes are generally less deceptive. It is there-

fore a very safe shot to play an attacking clear to your opponent's backhand and it may result in a half-court reply. I specifically say attacking clear because if you hit a high clear then your opponent may have time to play the return from the round-the-head position which can be both powerful and deceptive. If your opponent is covering the backhand side well then it may be necessary for you to play a number of shots first, perhaps a drop to the forehand before delivering the attacking clear to the backhand. The positions of these two shots are shown in the diagram.

The higher the standard of play the more common it is for your opponent to have a weaker forehand than backhand. This weakness often arises from the common fault of letting the shuttle drop much lower before returning it from the forehand baseline as opposed to the backhand baseline. If this is the case, an attacking clear to the forehand becomes a safe shot which may produce a half court lift or loose reply.

Safety-style tactics

Without question cutting down on errors, both forced and unforced, has to be an important goal for the ambitious singles player. How can you achieve this aim? Much can be gained by concentrating on playing safe

By following some simple rules a singles player can greatly reduce the number of unforced errors in his or her game.

shots. It is true that many points are lost directly off service and that generally a mistake comes within four or five strokes being played. It is therefore useful practice to concentrate on playing every shot safe for at least five strokes or until your opponent makes a mistake. This sounds fine in theory, but how do you play safe? The diagram above shows the areas of the court that can be considered safe. The strokes that are used, in detail, are:

1 Clears down the centre of the court or down the centre of each side of the court which land just beyond the doubles back service line.
2 Slow overhead drops and mid-court blocks to just beyond the front service line.
3 Smashes to just in front of the back service line safely two yards inside the side line.
4 Fast drops and half smashes to mid-court.

By hitting shots well within the court you are less likely to make a mistake. More importantly your opponent will find it very difficult to play a tight net shot for example, from a shuttle taken behind the front service line, and it is impossible for your opponent to create an angle from a clear directed to the centre of the backcourt. Such tactics are often used by the famous Danish player Morten Frost, several times winner of the Masters and All England titles. Morten has an immaculate defence, particularly from his backhand wing, and therefore he can feel comfortable in lifting well within the base line knowing that no player in the world can consistently hit through him.

Safety-style tactics can be useful at all levels and in order to give yourself a good chance of defending successfully, look carefully at the photograph of Morten Frost's defence stance. In a good singles defence stance the racket should be held out in front of your body, pointing towards the backhand side and using the backhand grip. By holding the racket out in front of your body you can defend shots directed to your body using the backhand grip and it is easy to change the position of the racket to cover the forehand side if necessary. Hold the racket at around waist height with your knees slightly bent.

Many unforced errors come from the return of the high service. The best safety replies to such a service are a high clear reply directed to the centre of the backcourt mid-way between the tramlines or, preferably, an attacking clear directed to the centre of one side of the court just beyond the back service lines. A drop reply is better performed as a sliced drop in a position just past the front service line and perhaps a yard inside the side line. A slow drop is a dangerous shot and often loses the point. In practice sessions imposing a penalty of, say, 10 sit-ups is useful in deterring the ambitious player from making errors off service. A full smash directed down the centre of the court is also a safe shot but can become dangerous when played from a really good high service dropping vertically just inside the back line.

A safe reply to a well-executed low service is a flat and fast lift to the straight corner yet safely inside the line boundaries.

A safe reply to a flick service is a smash at least a yard inside the side line or an attacking clear but again well within the line boundaries.

Talbot's tips

Given the choice of ends at the start of a match, if there is a difference in sides then always choose the worst end first. It is better to finish a match from the best side of the court. In the first game, when none of the players are fully settled, it is less of a disadvantage to play at the worst side. The quality of ends is usually governed by the background but other factors such as lighting or spectators may need to be taken into account.

Attacking-style tactics

Some players are natural defenders and make safety style tactics their basic bread and butter with only short bursts of attacking play. However, others are natural attackers and these players usually find they make few errors from smashing the shuttle. This becomes a well-used ingredient in their play interspersed with occasional patches of safety play to break up the game. I believe that both styles of play should be encouraged. Although singles is undoubtedly a game of limiting the errors, the attacking style enjoys more than its fair share of success and players with this talent should be encouraged to blossom. Of course there is a lot more to this approach than smashing the shuttle.

In the attacking game there is greater use of the short service. This is played for a number of reasons.

The receiver has to play either to the net or lift the shuttle in some way or other. A return to the net is countered by another net shot inviting the opponent to lift the shuttle or by a flat push to the back of the court inviting a fast flat reply.

A lift by the opponent from the short service gives an attacking player the opportunity to pressurize the opponent with a smash, a sliced drop or an attacking clear. Such fast shots give

the opponent less time to think of the best reply and quite often force an error. It must not be thought that such dominance of the net and the proliferation of fast attacking shots automatically assumes that the attacking player is looking for an early winning shot. This is rarely the case in top class play. Obviously if the opportunity is there to score a point it will usually be taken but there are many times when an attacking player is pressurizing the opponent to such a degree that the opponent is working anaerobically (the muscles are using up their store of energy rather than operating on the oxygen the player is breathing). Therefore it is a better tactic to prolong such a rally. It is important to understand that the singles match isn't over in a few minutes and that winning a few quick points does not mean that the match is won. Nevertheless the point of the game is ultimately to get the shuttle on the floor and an opponent with a fearsome attack can be a worrying foe. The safety-style player may try to tire, bore, depress or mentally break the opponent down but if the attacking player has too much fire-power then such a tactic may be futile. A top class match between these contrasting styles provides the ultimate spectator experience, the outcome of which is rarely easy to predict.

Two good replies to a short service.

Two very good replies to a short service for the attacking style player are the net shot and flat push to the rear of the court.

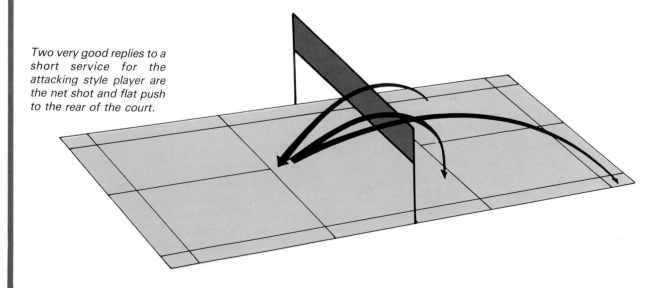

The even doubles game

The attacking formation

When a pair is in the attacking formation one player is covering the back of the court and the other is covering the net. The photograph shows such a formation which is preferable when the players are forcing their opponents to lift the shuttle. Such a formation is particularly vulnerable to a push down the side of the court to a half court position. Often both players are undecided as to who should play the shot.

There are many forms of attack beyond a smash. The player at the back of the court may drop, half smash or drive the shuttle, all of which would be considered to be attacking shots. Also the net player may play a net shot, half court push, flat push to the back of the court, brush shot down the centre of the court or block shot, all of which would also be considered as attacking shots. The attacking shot is one which puts the opponent on the defence and forces them to lift the shuttle. It does not need to be a hard hit shot. Attacking shots are generally hit by the opponents when they are travelling in a downwards direction.

Below: on the attack with a serve from the rear of the court. The server's partner stands just behind the front 'T' to intercept the reply if possible.

Left: The attacking pair are directing a smash down the centre of the court against a typical side by side defensive formation.

Below left: The half court push can be very defensive against an attacking formation. The area of the court marked X is suf ficiently far away from both opponents.

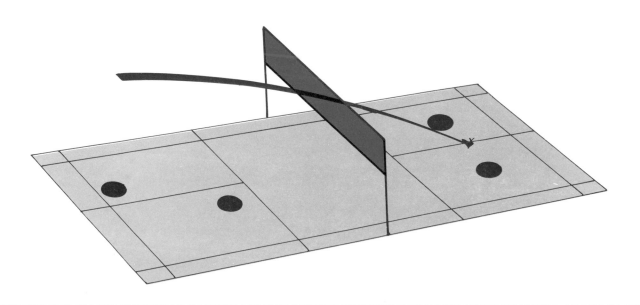

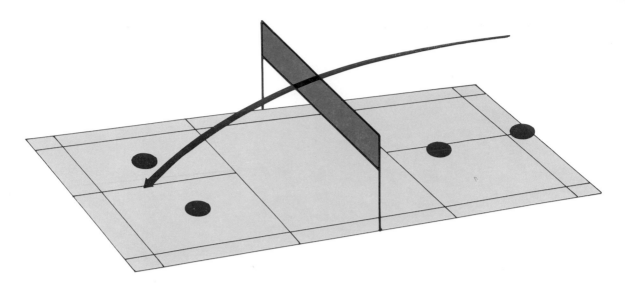

Above: The defensive formation on the left is vulnerable to attacking shots directed down the centre of the court.

Below: This is an example of playing under pressure. Occasionally, players are forced to defend in the front and back positions as shown here instead of the more usual side by side formation.

The defence formation

Here the players are side-by-side with one player approximately in the centre of one half court while the other player is in the centre of the remaining half court.

This is an ideal formation to cover a well hit smash but it is easy to see that a shot played to the net is largely uncovered and one directed down the centre of the court may leave the pair undecided about who should play the shot. Half-court pushes against such a formation are likely to be less effective. Generally players in defence assume the backhand grip with the racket well out in front of the body and it is important that they should have an understanding as to who is going to cover smashes directed down the centre of the court. As a rule such a shot is covered by the player capable of returning the shot with a backhand stroke. Naturally when a right-handed player combines with a left-handed player an appropriate understanding must be agreed.

Change from attack to defence

The defensive play of most top players is so good that it is almost impossible to sustain a constant attack. Invariably a well-delivered smash is either blocked to the net or driven flat back past the player at the net, forcing the opponents to lift the shuttle themselves. Doubles rallies can be very exciting as the attack turns to defence

on numerous occasions throughout the rally and it becomes difficult to establish which pair has the initiative. In this war of attack and counter-attack often one fast flat return is dealt with by the delivery of a similar shot back. Such play demands extremely fast reflexes and a very fast racket action. Such shots are common today, mainly because of the lightness of rackets available. It would have been almost impossible to play in this manner with the relatively heavy wooden racket of days gone by.

The flat return is executed with the racket held well out in front of the body with the backhand grip. By holding the racket like this it is possible to cover shots to the forehand still maintaining the backhand grip.

Fast flat exchanges are often won by the player who first takes the pace off the shuttle and plays a block to the net. It is easy to be caught up by the pace of the rally and to forget about playing a soft shot. The ability to vary the pace of strokes within a rally is a simple but effective strategy in doubles play.

Left: A player defending a smash directed across the body, using a backhand grip, by holding the racket well in front of the body.

Service tactics

As described in Chapter Two on the rules of badminton you cannot win a point unless you are serving. However, it is amazing how many errors are made on service by players of all levels, thereby throwing away the chance of scoring a point.

Successful doubles combinations consistently deliver a good low service. This service is most important as the receiver cannot play a positive shot. If the receiver finds it easy to return a short service delivered to the centre of the court with a positive shot then the server must vary the point at which the shuttle crosses the net until an effective short service direction is found.

It is a simple tactic to vary the short service yet it is amazing how many players will continue to deliver the same service even though it is dealt with mercilessly by the receiver.

Below: A successful return of service may be the block, the half-court push or brush, and the flat push to the back of the court.

Generally, a service wide to the side of the court is the most difficult to rush. As usual, the best tactic is to force your opponent to lift the shuttle.

Only in order to surprise an opponent or if all variations of short service are unsuccessful should you resort to the flick or high service. There are some doubles combinations, whose defences are strong enough to cope with their opponents' attack, who may decide upon the tactic of lifting the shuttle, actively inviting the opponent to attack. While this can on occasions be successful it is an extremely dangerous tactic to use as a general rule.

Return of service tactics

There are three main returns to a good short service. These are the block, the half-court push or brush, and the flat push to the back of the court. These returns are shown on the diagram.

Returns of a good short service

A simple block to the net is a very effective reply to the short service. If the server is effectively covering the court, a deep push down the side of the court is a good tactic.

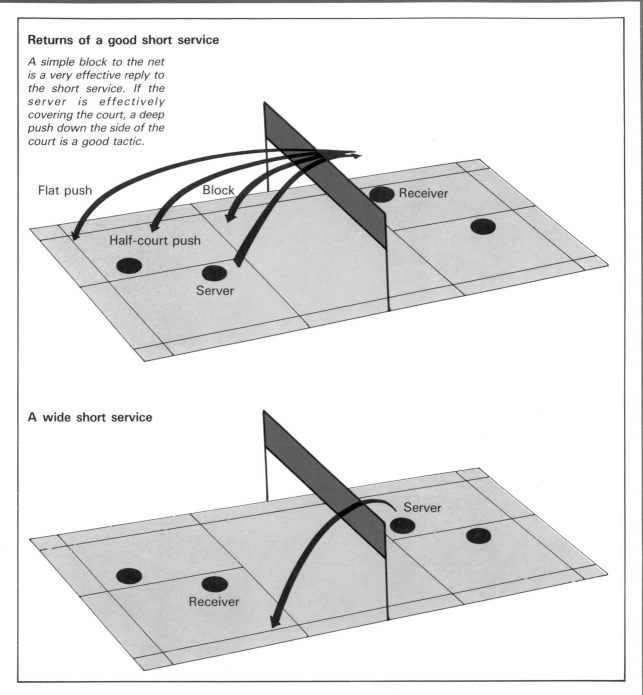

Flat push

Block

Half-court push

Receiver

Server

A wide short service

Server

Receiver

The risk in playing a block or net shot return is that the server may anticipate the net reply and be able to step forward and kill the shuttle from the top of the tape. A flat push to the half court is a safer shot, providing the trajectory of the push is downwards — an early interception by the server could be disastrous. If the service is very tight over the net then the flat push to the back of the court, preferably to the backhand corner, is the safest return. The trajectory can be very flat if the receiver takes the shuttle early as it crosses the net. A useful tactic is for the server to try and anticipate all replies by the receiver which can intercepted early. If by such good play on the part of the server the receiver is forced to push every reply to the back of the court, then the server's partner will have a better chance of anticipating and hitting an early effective reply.

Covering the net

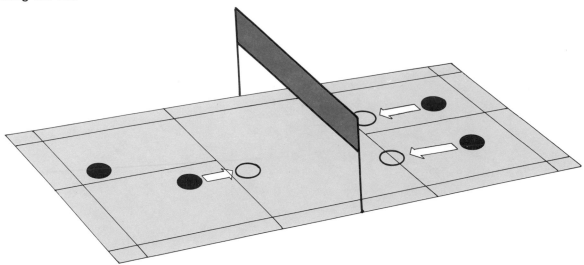

Above: Tap action can be played to great effect by the net player to kill from the net and produce fast flat pushes to the half court and rear court.

Below: It is essential never to leave too large a gap at the front of the court which at all times must be covered by one member of the partnership.

Role of the net player

It is extremely important that at all times there is a player ready to cover the net. It is all too common to see players in the defensive formation standing too far back in the court thereby leaving a huge gap at the front. This gap is a safe target area for the opposing pair as they know any shot played to this area cannot be intercepted and inevitably the resulting reply will be a lift. Thus the attacking pair can safely continue their attack.

Generally in any combination one player should be good at playing in the forecourt whilst the other should be better able to play in the rear court. If so the net player must be alert for shuttles played to the front of the court. Obviously it is important for the net player to be competent at the back of the court in the same way as the rear court player needs to be competent at the net. Nevertheless such an ideal combination rarely exists and a useful basic tactic therefore emerges

whereby the net player is forced to play at the back of the court and the rear court player is forced to play at the net. This can be achieved by serving short to the rear player and flick serving the net player. Obviously there are many other variations during the rally which can bring this simple but effective tactic into play.

So what is the net player expected to do? Well firstly you must always be alert and in an appropriate stance ready to intercept at the earliest opportunity when your partner is attacking from the back of the court. The net player's position of readiness is shown in the photograph.

The net player must be capable of playing the tap action to great effect. This action is necessary to kill from the net and produce fast flat pushes to the half court and rear court. Good reflexes are an essential ingredient of the net player. If there is one single message for the net player it is always to play a shot which will give your side the attack, and knock the shuttle off the net at every opportunity.

Above: The net player is alert with racket up in front of the body, ready to intercept whenever possible the return to his partner's smash.

Talbot's tips

If your opponent is on a winning streak never allow him to rush you. If he tries, make an extra effort to collect the shuttle from the net and do not pass it back to him until you are in a position to receive service. Never worry about wiping your brow or taking a few extra seconds to settle into your receiving position.

Role of the rear court player

The player at the rear of the court is in a position to attack the shuttle that has been lifted. Where in the court should the attack be directed?

The smash

If A lifts the shuttle to C then the safest, most effective smash for C to play is one to the forehand of A. The main reason for this is that in general A will be adopting a backhand defensive position and a smash across his body to his forehand will force him to move his racket arm to cover the smash. The angle of return is reduced and any reply to the smash has the best possible chance of being intercepted by C's partner D who is standing just to the left of the centre of the forecourt. D is standing just to the left because if C smashes to A's backhand then a fast cross court reply must be intercepted by D. The other reason why a smash to A's forehand is the safest and most effective shot is

A cross-court smash can be effective if directed across the body to the opponent's backhand but great accuracy is required.

that if C places the smash in error a little to either side of the target area then the result is still a good smash. A smash slightly to the right will result in a smash to A's body, still a very effective shot. An error to the left will result in a smash down the centre of the court which is also an effective shot.

In the diagram if A lifts the shuttle to C it is an extremely dangerous shot to smash cross-court to B's backhand. As we can see it is relatively easy for B to whip a backhand across to a position X which will bypass D and leave C with a lot of ground to cover and undoubtedly the shuttle will be near to the floor if D is able to reach it.

If, in the same move, C can smash accurately enough across the body of B then B has to change from a defensive stance covering the backhand to a suitable position to cover the forehand. Such a move can be awkward and a loose return gives D the chance of an interception. It must

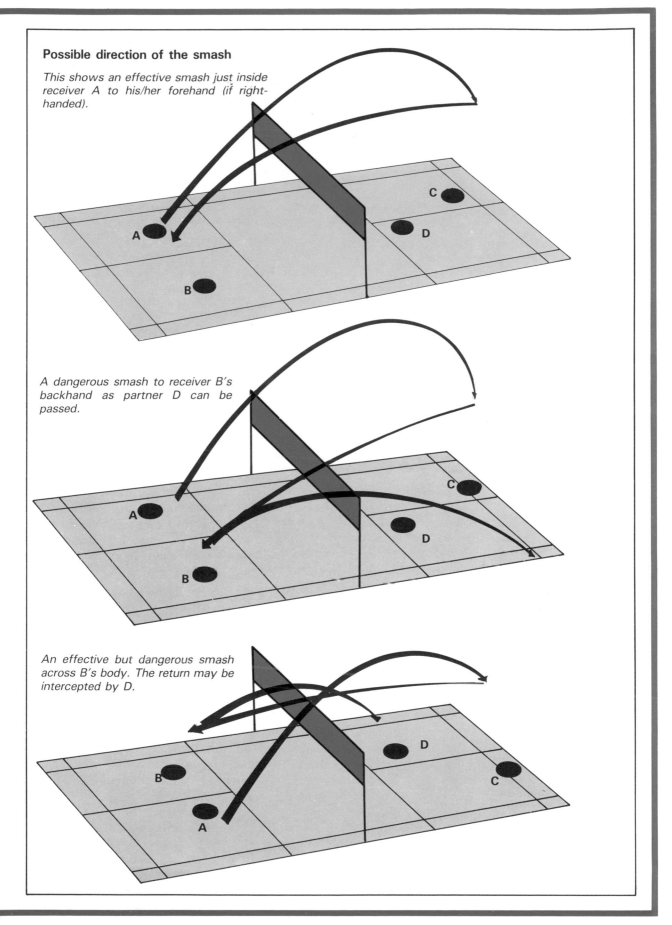

Possible direction of the smash

This shows an effective smash just inside receiver A to his/her forehand (if right-handed).

A dangerous smash to receiver B's backhand as partner D can be passed.

An effective but dangerous smash across B's body. The return may be intercepted by D.

Above: Caught back on their heels against a well delivered half-smash attack.

Opposite: A typical jump off the ground to add power and/or angle to the attack.

be stressed however that most club players do not have the desired degree of accuracy in their smash to do this. Also it is essential that there is an understanding between the pair so that D knows that partner C may deliver such a shot. This smash is particularly effective from the backhand court across court to the backhand of a right-handed player. Nevertheless it must be stressed that this is not a safe shot and must be used sparingly.

The half-smash attack

If an attacking player is finding it difficult to penetrate with a full smash then the half smash can be very effective. By slicing through the shuttle the resulting spin affects the trajectory allowing the shuttle to fall with less pace more steeply over the net. Half smashes are often difficult to defend. If the receiver is standing too far back into court then it is impossible for the receiver to take the shuttle early enough to play a flat return and change

the opponent's attack to defence. Alternating between a series of full smashes to a series of half smashes makes it difficult for the opponents to find a comfortable base.

The drop attack

The drop shot can be used to great effect when the defending couple occupy a base too far back into court. A deceptive drop shot delivered when the opponents are expecting a smash often provides an easy winner. A useful tactic is to smash flat to force an opponent into taking up a base position well back into court then to follow up with a drop shot into the open fore-court. Slow drop shots, which are anticipated, can easily be killed at the net or dealt with in a positive manner. Such anticipation can be, to some extent, prevented by the use of a sliced drop shot which travels to its destination more quickly. The use of a sliced drop is a very effective safe shot to play when attacking.

The drop attack

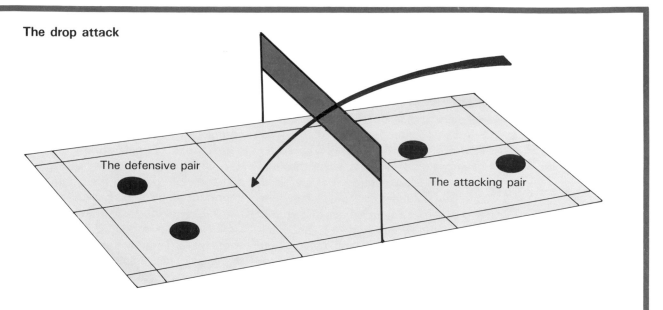

The defensive pair

The attacking pair

The mixed doubles game

Badminton is one of only a few sports able to boast as many women players as men. It has developed through a network of clubs where mixed doubles is the predominant game and it has been fostered over the years through numerous local leagues. The standard of mixed doubles has always been high and indeed Europeans have shown the rest of the world some of the great variations of strokes and tactics that make mixed doubles a fascinating game.

Mixed doubles formation
Normally the lady player has responsiblity of the net while the man covers the back of the court. There are many variations between the two roles and indeed in a few cases they are completely reversed. However, the general rule is largely observed.

This formation is an attacking one and therefore perhaps the single most important tactic is to attack. As neither pair wishes to lift the shuttle high in the air there is a predominance of flat shots, played mainly down the sides of the court. There is also a need to gain dominance of the net. Let us look at the roles of the girl and the man separately and analyse the tactics which emerge from some of the most important moves.

Below and opposite: Mixed doubles — the 'bread and butter' event of the sport, and which shows the greatest variation of tactics and racket skills.

The role of the girl

It is most important for the girl to have a good short service, good enough to prevent a positive 'rush' from either the opposing man or girl. The same principles apply as for even doubles only flicks and high services should be used even more sparingly as they automatically give away the attack. It must be said however that at club level it is often an effective tactic to serve high to the girl as this draws her away from the net and many girls are not strong enough to play a positive reply. As a general rule the girl in this situation should smash or half smash the service, following her shot in to cover the net.

If girl B serves high to girl C then C's best shot is a straight smash which will be returned by A. Her movement into the net after the smash should not be so fast as to make it easy for A to return the smash over her head yet she must be able to deal with a straight block from A to the net. Her partner D will have to take any cross court reply or indeed a really high return of the smash over her head. At international level C may be strong enough overhead to stay out if A returns high into the air but generally this is a dangerous move and one which the opposing man A would normally relish. It would be dangerous for C to return her smash cross-court as there would be a good chance of an early interception by opposing girl B.

In the above example man D is in a position to help his partner out at the net. This is very important for it is a common fault for the girl to try and cover the whole net during a rally. To attempt to do so she would need to position herself at the centre of the net around the short service line and such a position leaves large gaps to her forehand and backhand providing easy target areas for the opposing man. She would be run from side to side by an opponent of reasonable skill. In order to be effective at the net her ability to anticipate must be good but equally she must try to anticipate and make a definite commitment to her side of the net. It is then her partner's job to cover the remainder of the net should she anticipate wrongly. This puts a tremendous degree of pressure on the opposing man who knows that if the girl at the opposite side of the net anticipates his shot then it will have to be tight over the net in order not to be killed. The necessity for such accuracy brings about errors.

The opposing man realizes that at least one side of the net is going to be covered but it is important that he is unsure which. To achieve this doubt the girl must be able to look as though

The straight smash return to a high service

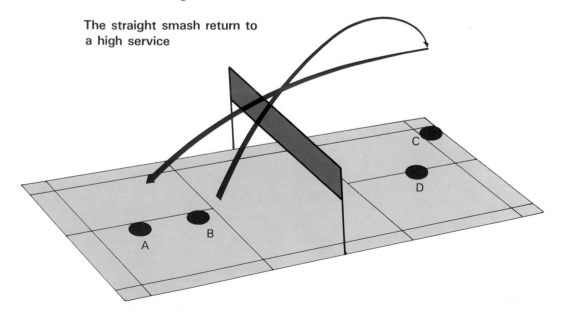

she intends to stand still then move swiftly to the reply. Alternatively she must also be able to look as though she intends to move but in the event stands still. Such talent demands a great deal of practice but without the knowledge of the art achievement is impossible.

When a pair is forced to lift the shuttle the girl must be capable of taking the cross-court smash. To do this effectively she must quickly calculate whether the lift is deep enough to make a steep smash pos-sible. If so she can move forward to the front service line with racket up, knees bent, and either block or tap the smash, depending on the pace of the shuttle. If, however, the lift is short then she must retreat from the net, adopt the backhand grip and stand sufficiently near to the side of the court to make a smash across her body diffi-cult or impossible. The smash straight down the centre of the court becomes the responsibility of her partner. The diagrams show the different approaches to the cross-court smash.

Below: An effective straight smash reply by a girl to a high or flick service.

The role of the man

The man in the mixed doubles partnership must be able to have great accuracy with his smash. Not only does his attack need to be accurate but he needs to be able to vary the pace and angle of smash through the total spectrum of possibilities. Choosing the right type of smash is a great talent and its placement can mean the difference between playing for your partner or cutting her out of the game completely. Smashes directed down the centre of the court are more likely to produce returns which can be intercepted by the lady partner. The cross-court smash can so often cut the girl out of the rally totally.

The ability to control the shuttle so that it passes tight over the net from all positions on the court is an important quality for a man. As the girl is in the main covering the net, any shot passing loosely over the net is likely to be put away. Shots which pass tight over the net are often directed to mid-court positions just beyond the reach of the girl covering the net. Indecision as to who should play these shots is commonplace. Many club-level ladies come too far off the net only to find that they are literally standing on their partner's toes leaving the complete court wide open for their opponents. So the tactic of tempting the girl off the net with half-court pushes is a good one.

Already discussed is the tactic of moving the girl off the net with a high service. This is another useful way of creating openings at the net to which a simple shot will often result in a lift by the opponents, giving the man the opportunity to smash.

In many of the moves in mixed doubles deception plays an important role, with the couple constantly trying to wrong-foot their opponents. Deception plays a greater role in mixed doubles than in any other area of the game of badminton.

Below: A good attacking formation forcing the lady opponent away from the net where she is least effective.

Opposite: An effective lunging movement taking the shuttle far out in front of the body.

Deception

There are many forms of deception involving either body movements, changes in racket direction or merely not doing the obvious, but essentially for deception to occur someone must be deceived. Deception and anticipation are linked. Players try to anticipate shots in order to give themselves more shot alternatives by getting to the shuttle early. There is a danger, however, of anticipating and moving before the shuttle has been struck, if the opponent is skilled in the art of deception.

There is a great satisfaction to be experienced in keeping an opponent guessing and then tempting him to go the wrong way from the direction of the shuttle. Sadly deception is a less used art in today's game than it was 20 years ago, when players like Finn Kobbero graced the courts and showed us all his bag full of tricks. While I would not deny the need for power, speed and fitness, winning a game on these factors alone leaves me feeling just a little empty.

Certainly in my book no player is complete without skill in deception and there can be little doubt that badminton with this facet is a more entertaining game to watch. Today many players are coached to the top and it is interesting that many could learn a lesson or two from hundreds of self-taught club players who trick their way through games in practice every week. So let us now look at the various forms of deception both from the viewpoint of the deceived as well as the deceiver.

Body deception

Body movement can enhance the chance to deceive and it is usually most effective when the movement is slight. Exaggerated movement rarely deceives. For example, when playing a net shot just a slight sway in the opposite direction to the intended direction of the shot can be effective.

Your opponent will often move the wrong way in an attempt to anticipate the shot giving you the best chance of preventing your opponent attacking your net shot.

If a shuttle is played well over your head you usually need to lean back in order to play a clear. This movement prior to playing a drop shot from such a position can be very effective.

In defending a smash to an open court from a deceptive player, moving to cover the target area prior to the opponent striking the shuttle and then moving back to your original position may cause the opponent to change his mind and hit the smash directly to you. This may be risky but if the target area is sufficiently large it may provide your best chance of rescuing the rally.

Taking the shuttle early

Perhaps the single most important factor in most forms of deception is to move to the shuttle early before making your choice of shot. As soon as your opponent sees your racket in the target area he will be trying to anticipate your shot. If you are able to make up your mind right at the last moment (just before impact) then any pre-conceived ideas your opponent has can possibly be wrong. Once your racket is in the target area your opponent should not commit himself to a particular movement or he will be most vulnerable to a deceptive shot to a difficult area of court. Letting the shuttle drop too low before finally striking it limits the number of possible returns and consequently your opponent's chance of anticipating your shot increases.

Neutral deception

This simple form of deception can be achieved by developing exactly the same stroke build-up for more than one stroke. In other words you may have exactly the same build-up for a smash and a sliced drop, or a sliced

drop and an attacking clear and so on. In this way you are presenting to the opponent a neutral picture making it impossible for that opponent to anticipate your stroke. Normally players who anticipate well do so because they read the signs shown by the opponent preparing to hit the shuttle. If there are no signs then anticipation, other than a guess, is impossible. It sounds very simple to develop this type of deception but in fact it is extremely difficult in practice. Nevertheless players wishing to improve their standards should attempt it, particularly in the formative years before bad habits take hold.

Players who develop unnecessary and superfluous stroke habits will find that they provide their opponents with sufficient information to enable them to interpret their play correctly and anticipate their intended moves early. Good technique is the clue.

Left: Brushing across the shuttle disguises the direction of the return to a high service.

Opposite: Christina Bostofte of Denmark concentrates hard on her single serve delivery.

future low serves and unlikely to 'jump' the service.

Service deception

We have already covered the short, flick and high service. If you are faced with an opponent who is rushing the short service to great effect usually you will find that he is moving just as you are hitting the shuttle (if not before, even although this is a fault). Slowing down but not stopping the action just before impact and then producing the flick service will often have the receiver moving forward to merely watch the shuttle fly overhead. At worst it will make your opponent less confident on

Return of service

The backhand brush can be very effective in returning a short service when the receiver prepares to play a backhand push deep to the opponent's backhand then at the last moment brushes across the shuttle playing it straight down the centre of the court. The opponent inevitably moves to cover the backhand and by being out of position often presents his opponent with a loose shot to the net. This is only one example of the use of deception in the return of service.

Left: A brush return to a short service directed down the centre of the court when the opponent is expecting a return to his backhand (if right-handed).

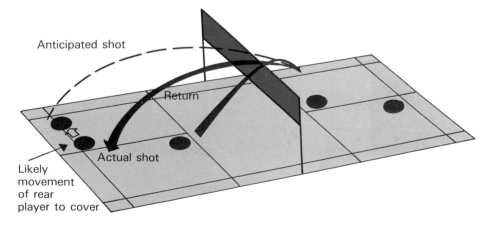

Anticipated shot

Return

Actual shot

Likely movement of rear player to cover

Racket deception

The player pretends to play the shuttle in a particular direction and then just before impact changes the path of the racket movement thereby altering the direction of the shot. In order to be effective in deception you must communicate to your opponent your intention to play a particular stroke and then you must smoothly change direction just prior to impact.

For example you may pretend to play a cross-court net shot and then at the last minue uncock your wrist to play a straight block. Rotating the wrist in such a manner is a skill which demands a lot of practice.

Another example would be to look

Below: Holding the wrist in a fully cocked position before a last second release of the wrist to produce a flick to the rear of the court.

as though the intended stroke was a straight block then, as your opponent moved forward, uncock your wrist rapidly to produce a flick over his head. There are numerous examples of changing from a full smash to a sliced smash, and so on but the essential ingredient is the control and use of your wrist. This control must be such that if your opponent is not fooled then you should be able to revert to the original shot. In other words there is no point in flicking over your opponent's head if he remains in position and does not start to move forward.

The backhand brush is an effective racket action in producing deceptive shots. Lady B plays a straight push to her opponent man C who has an open court for a cross-court reply shown by the dotted line. C positions himself to play this shot but at the last moment brushes across the shuttle thereby hitting it straight. The racket follow-through is in the same direction as it would have been for the expected shot shown by the dotted line, which makes the actual shot particularly deceptive. The aim is to tempt the girl to move in anticipation of a cross-court reply and, even if she does not, the resultant shot is quite safe. More particularly, if you find your opposing girl stands still on such an occasion, then the next time this situation arises you can actually play the cross-court reply. Such deception is a vital factor in good mixed doubles play.

Not doing the obvious

This is the simplest from of deception and quite often the most effective. If in a game between A and B, B plays a short lift to A, B is under threat of a smash from A. B prepares for the smash by moving his base back only to be the victim of a drop from A. In producing this drop A must prepare for the stroke as though a smash was intended and then just before impact check the follow through of the racket head. In a different example, where a drop would be the obvious shot then perhaps an attacking clear would be the least expected and therefore effective shot.

It is necessary in all these examples for the player using deception to present a clear picture to the opponent and allow sufficient time for that opponent to interpret the picture before bringing the alternative shot into play. We often see players making so many movements of the racket head that the opponent is confused and merely stands still. The opponent is then presented with a gift, the so-called deceiver wondering why the opponent hasn't moved.

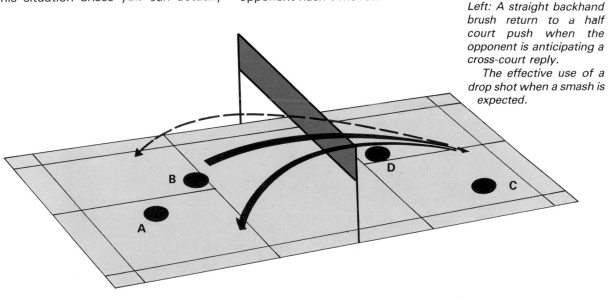

Left: A straight backhand brush return to a half court push when the opponent is anticipating a cross-court reply.

The effective use of a drop shot when a smash is expected.

Chapter 7 **Mental Strength**

The aim of this chapter is to offer direction to those readers who do not believe sufficiently in themselves to get the best from their own ability. It will also offer the positive thinkers guidelines to improve further their overall performance. Badminton is very much a sport which exercises the mind as well as the body, which is a major factor behind its worldwide appeal. Mental capabilities are closely linked to tactics and indeed we need to look at the complete mental approach before, during, and after the match.

Preparing for the match

Firstly it is normal to get pre-match nerves and indeed it is no bad thing. Interviews with many world-class athletes have proved that most are nervous before their event and several world record holders reported feeling particularly poorly prior to setting their world records. So regard these pre-match butterflies as part of the game and accept them as an important part of your enjoyment and success.

Breathing exercises
Composure, however, is essential and here breathing exercises will certainly help. You should breathe in through your nose and blow out gently through your mouth. Breathing must be from your diaphragm or stomach, to maximize the supply of oxygenated blood to the brain, which will reduce tension. It is necessary to keep your stomach extended at all times when breathing in and out. Your chest must not fully expand as this reduces the breathing from the stomach.

Positive thought
It is important that you get into the correct frame of mind. You must approach the game with a positive attitude towards winning but also with the contentment that having prepared in the best possible manner there will be things to learn, win or lose. You must never lose sight of the fact that it is a game. It should be fun above all else, and more enjoyable because of the satisfaction of having approached the task thoroughly. Once you have learned the strokes, the tactics, the movement and prepared yourself physically, you must learn to understand yourself.

Understanding yourself
It is important that you know your strengths and weaknesses in order to prepare a satisfactory game plan against a given opponent. If it is possible you should watch your opponent in a prior match to discover any weaknesses and to remember any favourite

Far right: Christina Bostofte regrets a missed point. There are moments when such expressions are unavoidable. What really matters is the player's ability to respond with both calm and determination.

shots. Having the ability to return effectively an opponent's favourite shot can be extremely useful in destroying their confidence. In order to understand yourself and to understand your opponent you should ask yourself the following questions:

1 Are they good at net play?

2 Do they prefer to play cross court net shots?

3 Is the forehand or backhand stronger?

4 Can your opponent's clears be intercepted?

5 Can your opponent play round the head when in the backhand court?

6 Do they stand up to concentrated clears to forehand or backhand?

7 Can they clear to the base line with both forehand and backhand?

8 Can your opponent stretch forward comfortably to sliced drops and half smashes?

9 Is the defence stronger on the backhand or forehand wing?

10 Do they generally flat smash or slice smash?

11 Do they make errors off a short service?

12 Do they make errors off a flick service?

13 Do they make errors off a high service?

14 Do they defend well off the body?

15 What are their favourite shots?

There are many other questions to be asked. Perhaps you can think of some additional questions which would help your game. Such a simple factor such as whether your opponent is right- or left-handed is often only discovered after losing several points. The permutations are more complex when considering a particular doubles combination but the principles are exactly the same.

With good preparation you can go into a match content, but nevertheless you cannot afford to switch off mentally.

Mental approach during the match

Making a game plan

You should go into a match with a complete knowledge of yourself. You should have in your mind a game plan if you have studied your opponent. If this has not been possible then you should use the knock-up to analyse your opponent and during this brief period should formulate a basic game plan. Obviously it is impossible to competely work out a player's style in two or three minutes of knocking up. The first few minutes of the match are therefore essential to further analyse your opponent.

Below: Darren Hall, a great competitor, has a victory smile as he holds aloft the coveted English National Singles trophy.

As the match progresses the game plan may have to be amended. For example, if you have decided to play an attacking style of singles then it is quite possible that, while this can be a successful game plan, your opponent may have a particularly effective reply to your short service. If so, you must change to a flick or high service while maintaining your attacking style during the rallies. The application of tactics and the ability to change tactics is an essential process of the mind.

Coping with tension

If tension is creeping into your game then stomach breathing will help you to relax (see page 124). This is particularly important at crucial points such as setting and match point. Many players do not know how best to approach crucial points within a match, such as changing at eight in a third game, or indeed any point of psychological importance, when it is vital not to make a silly mistake. The right tactics at such a point should not involve any risk shots and, while it may be prudent to maintain pressure on your opponent, this should never involve smashing for the line or playing for the tape at the net. This is the time for playing safely into court. When your opponent recognises that you are giving nothing away he is more likely to play risk shots himself and risk shots invariably produce errors.

The effects of fatigue

The analysis of a simple match becomes more and more difficult the longer the game goes on. As a player gets more fatigued the supply of oxygenated blood to the brain is reduced and sound reasoning is more difficult. When a player gets really tired certain mannerisms emerge and it is necessary to recognise them. In such a condition a player may scratch his head, walk continuously round in small circles between points, put his hands on his hips, and so on. When you see these signs it is important that you give your opponent no opportunity to rest. The ensuing rally must go on and on whether you are working aerobically or anaerobically. If you try to up the pace too much, to push your opponent into the anaerobic mode, then you might make a mistake, providing your opponent with an opportunity for a rest.

Also it may not be a good idea to take an easy winner in a close encounter unless victory is imminent. If you are the player who is tired then you must maximize your rest period in between rallies. This can be done by picking up a shuttle from the net and holding it in your hand until reaching your position to receive the next service before passing it back to your opponent. This makes rushing or hustling by the opponent difficult. Checking your shoelace is a certain give-away that you are feeling tired. It may be less obvious to walk up to the umpire and ask him to repeat the score or adopt a similar less common tactic rather than merely asking for a new shuttle. Even at the very highest level players do not exercise their mind sufficiently in this regard.

Communication

In doubles play it is important that you have communication with your partner. Encouragement at crucial points can bring out the best in a player. Such encouragement is important also when a player is going through a bad patch. We all know what it is like to have everything go wrong for a while and a sympathetic pat on the back from a partner can be all that is necessary to break the bad run. If you notice an important tactical point it is essential that you inform your partner at the earliest opportunity. The real benefit of such knowledge will not be achieved if you wait until after the game, or even worse, if you never discuss the tactic at all. Excessive talking gives the impression that you are worried and therefore it is essential to get just the right degree of rapport between partners. If you feel you are too tense, a smile across the net works wonders.

breathing a simple smile across the net will work wonders.

Positive thoughts

The secret is you have to learn to enjoy the tense moments in a match and approach these moments with a positive mind. There is a world of difference when the opponent is serving to you at 17 all if you think positively. 'If I can win this rally I can win the match with my service,' is the right way to think. 'If he wins this point he will have won the match,' won't help at all. You must practise thinking positively at every moment when negative thoughts come into your mind.

Above: Fiona Smith wins the English National Ladies Singles title. She is well-known for her good match temperament.

Talbot's tips

Always remember your opponent is human and therefore can be beaten. Even the best of players has weaknesses and these weaknesses can be exploited. Whatever the score never stop looking for the solution to a winning formula: You can if you think you can.

Mental approach after the match

If you go into a match having prepared fully, having tackled the game in a positive, thoughtful manner, then win or lose it should have been a pleasant experience. Of course it is only natural to feel a degree of disappointment if you have lost but what is most important is that you learn something, whatever the outcome, and that you come out of the encounter a better player.

Remember the match

If you have been applying the right thought processes during the game, you will have a mental picture of the complete match. You must analyze this picture to establish how you won points and how you lost points. It is necessary to remember the sequence of shots which led up to the final stroke, for it may be the second or third last stroke move which caused the problem or the success. In other words, if you were losing points on your defence it may be that these errors occured because of short lifts and therefore it is the lifts that require attention and not the defence.

Self-analysis

From analysis you will be able to discover your weaknesses and strengths. With this knowledge you are better equipped for future games to be able to cover up your weaknesses and force your opponent to play to your strengths. For example, if you find you win many points by playing

Below: Ib Frederiksen of Denmark jumps for joy as he wins against Morten Frost in an All England Final.

net shots and you have particular confidence in this department of the game, then introduce a high proportion of short services, slow drop shots and attacking clears to your opponent's backhand. This is likely to provide you with the opportunity of playing a net shot. If, through self-analysis, you find you lose many points from your backhand deep in the court then it would be sensible for you to concentrate play to your opponent's backhand (if also right-handed) as any replies to your own backhand will have to travel the longest distance across court, giving you more time and the best possible chance of intercepting the shot with your round-the-head forehand. Such tactics will help cover up weaknesses but there is no substitute for taking time to practise to improve those weaknesses. In the case of a weak backhand deep in the court then practising a fast backhand drop which also travels well into court may be a solution to get you out of trouble.

Enjoy the challenge

Approaching a match in this manner should be a challenge and above all it should be enjoyable. Many players take every match too seriously, particularly junior players, to say nothing of their parents watching and criticising from the sidelines. The whole exercise of preparing, playing and correcting should always be fun albeit conducted in a totally professional manner. Don't ever forget that word 'fun' and if you are completely bewildered by a game situation a positive response would be to smile first and think of a solution.

Above: Morten Frost takes his turn to be triumphant against Steve Baddeley.

Left: Ib Frederiksen of Denmark shakes hands with Jens Peter Nierhoff, also of Denmark, the loser on this occasion.

Talbot's tips

While a professional approach is preferable, never get over-jealous, show a really bad temper or take the game too seriously. It is most important to enjoy all aspects of playing the game.

Chapter 8 **Coaching Fundamentals**

Below: It is vital for the coach to be able to communicate well with players. This means talking to them in easily understood terms at their level, and involving them in these sessions by asking them questions and getting their feedback.

Although this chapter is directed primarily at coaches, it should also be read by players. It is intended to be both thought-provoking and instructional and contains reference to aspects of coaching and player-development not always included in badminton coaching books.

Every coach should ask himself: 'Why do I coach?' Be honest in listing your motives. You will know whether they are good ones, or if you need to change your outlook. Is every coaching session an opportunity for your players to impress you — or for you to impress them? Have you the courage to get good players to give a good demonstration of a shot or practice if you cannot?

I believe that a sound philosophy for

life, work and play can be based on three things: enjoyment, improvement and achievement. If you *enjoy* what you are doing, you will continue to want to do it. If you enjoy coaching, you will pass your enjoyment on to your players. Enjoying practice must lead to *improvement,* which in itself motivates the player, as does the *achievement* that inevitably follows.

A coach's role changes as a player develops. The novice requires more instruction, but eventually all the experienced player may require is a mentor. The coach has to step back from being a teacher and become a counsellor. Get to know your players and learn to listen, not just to verbal communication, but to body language. If you listen to them, they will listen to you, and you will be able to get your message across.

It was probably Confucius who said: 'Tell me — I forget; show me — I remember; involve me — I understand.' Think of this when you communicate with your players, and get the balance right. Here are some rules.

How to communicate with your players

1 Talk simply. It is of no use speaking Swahili if your listeners have never even heard of Africa.

2 Instruct at the right level. It is no use talking about nuclear physics if your listeners want to know how to

change a plug.

3 Demonstrate what you mean. We see in pictures, not in words. A good demonstration repeated frequently is more likely to be absorbed and reproduced than a detailed set of verbal instructions.

4 Involve your players. Ask questions and get them to think for themselves. Are you afraid of becoming redundant?

5 As in so many other aspects of life, the key word for the coach is 'balance', which is not to be confused with compromise.

● Balance between being too strict and too relaxed.

● Balance between seriousness and humour.

● Balance between talking too much and being deaf and dumb.

Above: The good coach always demonstrates what he means to the players. Frequent repetitions will help ensure that movements, skills and instructions are absorbed.

Below: Players learn best from good demonstrations and seeing the shots and skills executed by their coach. Practice, when enjoyable, leads to improvement and subconscious reproduction of what is being demonstrated.

How to make your point more memorable and visually stimulating

1 The visual message. Create an image your players won't forget. Treat a group of players who need livening up to the 'Dead Jellyfish Syndrome'. Ask them to picture a dead jellyfish lying on a beach. When prodded, it quivers briefly before subsiding into an inert mass. Not a pretty sight! The players will soon get your drift.

2 Mnemonics. Invent memory aids for your players. They will be useful to you too. Below is an example of a mnemonic showing the attributes of a singles player.

D eception and dynamism
O bservation of opponent and environment
C onsistency — Concentration — Confidence — Commitment
L ength, rear court and forecourt
E arly to shuttle
A ccuracy — Aggression — Agility — Attitude
R ange of strokes — reflexes — Recovery — Relaxation
S peed — Stamina — Strength — Strategy

Within this acronym is another useful mnemonic device — alliteration. Ask your players to remember the three Ws: Which shot? Where to? What reply?

3 Use of words. Choose your words with care and be aware of the tone in which you utter them. Do you speak, bawl, or whisper? Ask a player to hit the shuttle hard and watch the knuckles go white as the grip tightens. You want a young player to play a gentle net shot. Do you yell: 'Hit it gently!', or whisper just the one word: 'Gently', before each attempt?

4 A coach can PEP up coaching sessions by employing:

P raise, genuine and well deserved
E nthusiasm, which comes from passionate belief in the game, yourself and your players
P resentation: use the three Vs: Vivid, Verbal, Visual.

Mental capacity

Regrettably, coaches are usually perceived by players to be people who are there to criticize and find fault. Of course, at times this is necessary, but the benefit of your wisdom will be more lasting if you involve the player in recognizing, diagnosing and correcting any weaknesses. Do this by asking questions or using video equipment for

Below: The good coach can help the player to recognize, diagnose and correct fauls in his/her game. But it is important to praise as well as to criticise and find fault.

feedback. And never forget the stimulation that *praise* can give when it is genuine and well deserved.

How often have you heard a player come off court and, sometimes even after winning, say: 'I played rubbish' — or worse? Ask your players to be explicit in self-criticism and they will learn to discover *for themselves* what their faults are and how to correct them. Self-motivation takes over. I suggest that they will think more of you as a coach and not less, if you give them a sense of independence and autonomy.

Talbot's tips

For parents and coaches reading this book I believe too much emphasis is placed on children winning. Such pressure from the sidelines not only produces bad behaviour but can deter children from continuing to play the sport.

Players can be taught many mental skills to enhance their performance:

Relaxation is probably the single most important mental skill. Mastering it is essential if the other skills mentioned below are to be used effectively.

Visualization Encourage the technique of using the imagination to rehearse, to build concentration and other positive skills and to reduce the effects of negative emotions.

Awareness Players should listen to their senses, particularly sight, sound and feel. Just being aware of tension in the body and negative thoughts in the mind will in itself be beneficial. Coach your players to substitute positive thoughts for negative ones.

Concentration The natural tendency of the mind is to wander. No-one can concentrate indefinitely. Relaxation periods, however brief, are vital. Get your players to use triggers or cues — such as fiddling with the racquet strings — to bring back the focus of their attention.

Above: Coaches encourage their players to listen to their body and their senses, and to substitute a positive attitude for a negative one.

Above: A coach should help motivate the player by setting short-, long- and medium-range goals for him/her. For example, short-range goals may involve simple, frequently repeated practice routines performed without error.

Your attitude to your players can change their attitude to the game. Players are not machines that you can programme to win. Don't concentrate on physical achievement to the point where you neglect the psychology of the game.

The need for mental training in sports is only now being recognized, yet it is no less important than physical training. Does not the mind control the body? How often have you heard of or come across players who are superb in practice sessions but fail dismally when it comes to the crunch, because they just go to pieces?

Once you have developed a player's aptitude for the game to its maximum, the only factor that can be improved is his attitude. Train your players to be positive from the beginning.

● Train a player to have inner confidence but not outward brashness. Belief in oneself comes from such things as fitness, success and having been there before.

● Give your players the right attitude of mind for the stage of the game. When in *defence* a player should not be thinking *offence.*

● Encourage basic good manners and honesty in dealing with opponents, umpires and officials. It is extremely easy for a player to get a bad reputation, and extremely difficult to get rid of one. All it takes is a couple of tantrums or disputed line calls.

Here are just a few examples of positive and negative attitudes. Make sure your players recognize which is which.

Positive	Negative
enthusiastic	mega-bored
cheerful	miserable
energetic	listless (dead jellyfish!)
confident	hesitant — self-doubt
winner	loser

Your own attitude as a coach can change someone's behaviour from negative to positive — try it!

Goal-setting

This is becoming more acceptable in business as in sport as a means of personal development. Goal-setting can be described as a dream with an action plan. In summary goals should be:

challenging	measurable
realistic	time-related
specific	positive
flexible	monitored

Goal-setting should involve long-term, intermediate and short-term goals.

● Process goals relate to improving performance and tend to be short-term.

● Product goals relate to competition targets and are more influenced by external factors, such as the ability of opponents.

● Individual and team goals should be determined by the players in consultation with the coach — not by the coach alone!

Get your players to give themselves ratings from 0 to 10 for present play and decide where they would like to be on the scale in, say, two months' time. Then plan and work on a suitable programme.

Some suggested areas for goal-setting are:

Stroke production	Physical skills	Mental skills
racquet/shuttle control	movement/ footwork	confidence
power play	stamina	concentration
touch play	speed	self-control
defence	flexibility	motivation
accuracy		commitment
deception		determination
consistency		

Potential danger areas for coaches

Motivation Acknowledge the difference between motivation, which is getting a player to do something because he wants to do it, and manipulation, which is getting a player to do something because *you* want him to do it.

Praise Mechanical praise becomes meaningless and devalues genuine praise.

Success If only winning is success, then we are all bound to fail at some time. Success is rather performing to the best of one's ability.

Winning We all like winners, but consider whether winning should be put first before your player's wellbeing.

Stereotypes Do you want to produce a series of computerized clones performing to perfection? What measure of unorthodoxy should be encouraged?

Fear Arises from worrying about losing, pressure from the expectation and demands of others, and an over-active negative imagination. An ego-driven coach, like an over-ambitious parent, can, often unwittingly, put tremendous pressure on a player. Learn to recognize your fears and ask yourself: 'What is the worst that could happen?'

Stress management Stress can be both helpful and harmful. It becomes harmful when you place expectations on a player that are far in excess of his capabilities. In fault correction, push-

Above: Developing physical skills and fitness are important goals for the player. The coach can help improve agility, movement, speed, flexibility and stamina with stretching and awareness exercises.

ing a player too hard can make things worse. However, being too laid-back in your attitude to the game can be equally detrimental to your player's performance — results can't be achieved without a certain amount of tension, as even champion-class players will agree. Learn to recognize which player needs winding up and which needs calming down. People differ.

Coach dependency You may be tempted to encourage your players to rely on you too much. Teach players to think for themselves — otherwise, how will they cope when you are not around? Encourage team spirit. Remember that every team is made up of individuals, each with his own personality and needs. Add to this list of examples other ways of building team spirit:

● Getting to know each other
● Collective goal-setting
● Laughing together
● Working hard together

Talbot's tips

In order to progress as a player it is important for goals to be set. These should be short, medium and long in term. Short-range goals can be simple practice routines such as 20 smashes without error. Medium-range goals may be to defeat a particular opponent. Long-range goals may be to play for a team, county or country. In setting goals always try to be realistic in addition to creating a challenge.

Content of a coaching session

This will depend on the age and level of ability of participants. To varying degrees you should include the following elements:

Variety Avoid boredom by changing practices. Bring in another coach or expert from time to time.

Stroke production Practise strokes from different areas of the court and link in tactical situations. At what stage is the stroke played in a game? Introduce it in such a context as soon as is reasonable.

Fitness Remember the need to build stamina, speed and strength. For young children this should be low-key, perhaps in the form of playground games. Try aerobic exercises to music.

Movement Devise practices involving footwork patterns as they occur in game situations, shadow badminton; and awareness exercises concentrating on, for example, moving smoothly, lightly, dynamically, keeping the racquet at the ready, and so on.

Mental training Perhaps include a brief session on relaxation or a discussion on concentration, attitude, game ethics, players' experiences in competitive situations, etc. Introduce subjects such as diet for sports or prevention of injuries.

Warm-up and warm-down Include flexibility exercises.

Games Give players the opportunity to experiment with what they practised earlier in the session.

County players can very usefully be allowed to spend 15 minutes in small groups brainstorming and resolving a particular problem of one of the group. It is remarkable what ideas flow from these sessions.

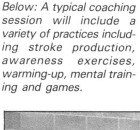

Below: A typical coaching session will include a variety of practices including stroke production, awareness exercises, warming-up, mental training and games.

Multi-player practices

When a coach has to cope with more than four players on a court there are several factors to consider.

S afety   The most important consideration. Join a coaches' register, which gives registered coaches automatic insurance coverage.

A ctivity   With some strokes it is possible to stagger players so that some play at the net and others at the rear of the court with a reasonable distance between them. Alternatively, organize the practice so that only one or two players run on to a court, play a shot and run off. Or arrange it so that while some players are on court, others are doing an off-court activity.

F un   To keep up the players' interest, practice must be fun.

E nergy   If players have to stand around, they soon get bored. Keep them all constantly involved.

There is a wealth of information on the physical, mental and social aspects of training, including books, audio cassettes and video tapes. I hope this chapter will encourage the coach to explore the subject further.

Above and left: In actual games, players can enjoy experiencing and putting into practice on court what they learnt earlier in the coaching session.

Talbot's tips

Ignorance of the growth phenomenon is also common in players under the age of 18. Here again the pressure to win can result in harmful training and practice programmes, which have a serious effect on the child's physical development. Resulting injuries can be both immediate and long term. Always consult an expert when working out a training programme for the under-18-year-old, as your responsibility to the player should never be overlooked.

Chapter 9 **The Experts' Game**

Ladies' singles *by Helen Troke*

I started my career at the age of 11, in a one court hall where you were lucky if you got a hit all night. On entering my first tournament, at the age of 12, I met my coach who told my mother I had potential. At this age I was very competitive but still learning the game. I became better and entered a few tournaments, getting hammered in most of them.

I worked hard at my game, became stronger, and won my first National title at 13 years old. I got my first cap for England at the age of 16 which made me the youngest player ever to play for my country.

One of the most memorable matches of my career was at 17 in the Commonwealth Games in Brisbane when I won the gold medal in the individual singles event. This was the time I really knew I could win when it really mattered. I then went on to win two European Championships and another Commonwealth gold.

The women's game has changed considerably in the last 12 years since I have been playing. We now have a Grand Prix circuit which means more tournaments around the world. Nearly every weekend of the year there is a Grand Prix tournament.

This makes it increasingly more difficult to peak for tournaments and to try to plan the programme sensibly to be able to cope with jet lag and acclimatization.

The standard of the women's game has improved since the Chinese women have been allowed back on to the circuit. They have made the pace of women's badminton much faster by hitting quicker shots. This is much more demanding for the person on the other side of the net, causing them to move faster. At this point in time, the Chinese women dominate the ladies' game. The only way to try and conquer them is to keep on playing them. This in itself is a challenge and an experience. It is knowing the right moment to play the right shot.

Fitness
Fitness training varies according to the individual's needs and the standard of play which is required by the player. My training is fitted around my on-court practice sessions and the demanding tournament schedules. The fitness which I feel is necessary for me to improve basically consists of training six days a week.

Flexibility
These are just basic stretching exercises done everyday before and after playing and training, to warm up the muscles and then to warm down and to help prevent injury.

Plyometrics
These are training drills which is designed to produce the explosive muscular power needed for badminton. The exercises require lots of jumping and bounding routines. The technique is to jump-land and take off straight away. They can be done over benches or cones, or by just hopping and bounding in a bit of space. It doesn't take very long for my legs to end up felling like jelly. I do these exercises once a week.

Running
Running is not really part of my training if I am building up to tournaments, but now and again I

Opposite: Helen Troke winning the final point in a match.

Above: Helen Troke in action performing one of her favourite shots — the 'round the head' smash.

Above: Helen Troke using the backhand grip is able to control a smash to the body.

abroad. It is excellent if you are stuck in a hotel with not a lot of room for training. Skipping usually takes 30 minutes, starting with ordinary skipping first, then going into double bumps for the last 15 minutes.

Shadow badminton

This is movement exercises where you practice the correct footwork of badminton on court without actually hitting a shuttle, but playing imaginary shots. They can be done as fast as you want, if you want to practice speed of movement, or as slow as you want if you need to learn new footwork routines. You can use all parts of the court or just specific areas. It does look ridiculous and people wonder what you are doing when performing these exercises, but I feel it is an important part of my training, being good for my fitness and footwork.

Routines — with a shuttle

These are numerous routines which I go through with my coach depending on which part of my game is not going too well or just needs working on. Usually we have a huge bag containing about 1000 shuttles which we work from. If we have a hard session the shuttles will be thrown or hit around the court with no mercy spared. I have to retrieve all the shuttles. Some rallies last what seems like hours, some are very quick, so this makes training into a game situation. Most of the routines we practice are based on game situations.

It is important in my view that coaching should be kept relatively simple and fun. The coach should be able to motivate the players in training and practice sessions. Five minute breaks in practice games are important between the second and third sets. I prefer to keep the break relaxed otherwise I go out and lose the next six points still thinking about what was said two minutes ago.

At any level coaching should be on a one to one basis, because I learn more and work harder. You can hide or

sometimes feel like running along the beach just to get my lungs going and to grab some fresh air. This is the fun part because it is done at my own pace.

Weights

Weights training is done a couple of times a week. I use heavy weights for my legs, which has the same effect as plyometrics and lighter weights for my arms.

Skipping

Most of the skipping is done when I go

slacken off in a group, but at the end of the day you only get out of any coaching or training what you yourself are prepared to put in. Why bother to cheat yourself — hard work is what it is all about.

Tactics

Try to find the strengths and weaknesses of your opponent by trying out various shots. When you have found these strengths and weaknesses try to use them to your advantage.

Here are some of the ways in which you can find out your opponent's weak spots:

1 Hit attacking shuttles to your opponent's body to see how good their defence is. Try to discover where they direct their replies. Do they whip them straight to the back of the court or do they block straight or cross court?

2 When attacking down the side wings of the court, are they quick to react and do they turn quickly to retrieve? If not, then hit half smashes and full smashes down the side wings of the court. If they are slow moving up and down the court then play drops and clears.

3 Find out if the player is weaker at the back of the court or at the net. Try to expose those weaknesses. If the weakness is at the back, then use the net area to exploit the rear court. If they are weaker around the net, hit slices and drops to bring them into the net to force them to play at the net.

4 Try to dictate the rallies by using deception. Hold shots for as long as possible to keep your opponent guessing. Make them wait so that they are always late reacting to the shuttle. Deliberately leave open areas in your side of the court to lure your opponent into hitting into an area, so you make them play the shots you want them to play. Always keep your opponent under the maximum pressure by killing any loose shots.

5 Bore your opponent by playing long rallies.

6 Increase the speed of the game.

7 Slow the game down.

8 Play a cross-court game.

9 Play a straight game.

10 Play deeper net shots (to stop your opponent spinning net shots).

11 Vary your serve. Perform a long, high serve, or a flick serve with pace, and also try a short serve to break the game up.

Mental approach

Make your opponent wait until you are ready. Use the time between rallies to recover breath and to gather yourself. Always be aware of your opponent's physical state. Chase every shuttle and never give up, the game can always change around.

Below: Helen, forced right to the back of the court, uses a long stride to get back to her central base position.

Men's singles *by Steve Baddeley*

Above: Steve Baddeley in action at full stretch on the backhand.

Above right: Steve Baddeley winning the English National Singles title.

Men's singles is a highly demanding activity involving a fascinating array of skills and qualities. Fleetness of foot and speed of hand are combined with balance and co-ordination; strength and power are allied with a delicate touch; quick-witted tactical decision-making is needed alongside patience, concentration and calmness under pressure; and stamina and endurance are needed to sustain these factors over periods of up to 90 minutes. I shall describe, here, the basic tactical strategy underlying my approach to this challenging sport.

I favour an attacking style of singles, preferring to hit the shuttle downwards into my opponent's court rather than allowing the reverse to occur. I have always been known for my powerful smash and my whole game plan has developed around this stroke.

I use my smash for two distinct purposes. Whenever possible, I smash an outright winner into a space left by my adversary. Many players save their smashes almost exclusively for this purpose. Opponents are moved around the court until they are out-manoeuvred and a gap appears into which the shuttle is smashed.

However, I regularly use my smash in another way too. I use it to create openings, not just to exploit them. Often I hit a smash knowing my opponent is on his base and likely to return it. My intention is to force a weak return which will give me the initiative in the rally.

What causes this weak return? Partly, it is a result of the fact that I hit the shuttle very fast — at speeds approaching 100 mph I am told. However, this is only part of the reason. If I practise my straight smashes with a fellow international player, it will normally take 10 or more powerful smashes before I can force him to hit a weak return. However, in a game situation I can frequently obtain a weak return off my first smash. This is because I have developed a lot of variation when I hit overhead shots and so my opponent can never be sure what to expect. It is the element of surprise engendered by employing a mixture of overhead attacking shots that is crucial to an effective smash.

The options available to me when I return a shuttle struck high to my forehand rear-court are:

Straight smash	Cross-court smash
Smash to body	
Flat smash straight	Flat smash cross-court
Fast drop straight	Fast drop staight reverse slice or normal slice
Fast drop cross-court normal slice	Fast drop cross-court
Fast clear straight	Slow clear straight
Fast clear cross-court	Slow clear cross-court
Slow drop straight	Slow drop cross-court

The shots on the left are those I use regularly in my game. Those on the right I play only rarely. I will look at some of those shots in more detail but the over-riding point is that the preparation for all these shots must be similar if deception is to be achieved.

Smash to body

This is a very effective shot as my opponent's return is impeded by his own body. If you have a reasonable smash I highly recommend trying this tactic. Fire some steep smashes at your opponent's knees while aiming other smashes towards his chest.

Flat smash straight

Smashes are usually best struck with as steep a trajectory as possible so forcing the opponent to move not only to his side but also quickly downwards. However, I have found that it is often effective to hit the occasional smash deliberately flat so that it would land (if left) in the back tramlines. This may catch your opponent out, as he will normally expect all fast shots to land in the mid-court or forecourt and will therefore be surprised by a shuttle shooting past him at waist height. However, a word of warning is needed. If your opponent does retrieve this smash it may be easy for him to return the shuttle to your cross forecourt which may leave you struggling.

Above: Steve Baddeley takes an early shuttle in an unorthodox way which is nevertheless effective.

Sliced fast drops

These are highly effective strokes for a number of reasons. Firstly, the racket head speed can be the same as for a smash but, as less energy is imparted onto the shuttle because it is struck obliquely, the shuttle will not travel as far into your opponent's court as the smash will. Secondly, because the shuttle travels fast, your opponent will have to react quickly to retrieve it. Thirdly, slicing the shuttle causes the racket head to travel in a different direction to the shuttle, creating highly effective deception. Finally, it is a relatively easy shot to play consistently because the racket head action is fast

Above: Steve Baddeley with a perfect forward lunge, allowing him to take the shuttle early and thereby maintaining the pressure on his opponent.

Slow drop

This is useful occasionally as it drags your opponent right into the net. It is rarely an outright winner and is more difficult to play than a fast drop. If your opponent anticipates the shot he may be able to take the shuttle very high at the net so take the advantage. For this reason, the cross-court slow drop is very rarely used in men's singles.

The secret of success as an attacking player is to develop and use a wide repertoire of attacking shots. By so doing you will enhance the effectiveness of each individual stroke. The threat of a fast drop forces your opponent to be ready to lunge rapidly forwards so enhancing the effectiveness of your fast clears. A powerful smash pushes your opponent back so making your fast drops more deadly. Each stroke individually is of limited use; but used in combination you can enjoy tying your opponent up in knots.

I find that when I am playing well I am able to dominate because my overhead strokes are limiting my opponent's replies. I am often able, therefore, to hit an attacking overhead stroke and then anticipate the return. The most frequent example is when a smash or fast drop forces a return to my forecourt area because my opponent has only just been able to get his racket head to the shuttle. He is thereby prevented from using his wrist and forearm to flick the shuttle back to my rear court. Therefore, as soon as I hit a good smash or fast drop I will move immediately to the forecourt. Here, if the shuttle is above net height, I can attempt a kill or, as is more usual, if the shuttle is below net height, I can play a tight tumbling net shot.

Similarly, if I hit an effective fast clear which passes my opponent so that he is unable to get his body behind the shuttle he will often play to my forecourt because it takes a lot of strength to clear a shuttle in this situation. Once again I can anticipate this return and so control the rally.

Many such patterns or sequences of shots can be identified which regularly occur at all levels of play. It is of great

and the shuttle is not aimed to land close to the net. For all these reasons this is a shot well worth developing. I would suggest the normal slice hit cross-court from your forehand side as the easiest to master.

Fast clears

These should not be neglected. One of my major faults when younger was to ignore the rear of my opponent's court when hitting attacking overheads. In my desire to attack, I was reluctant to hit any type of clear. However, the fast clear is, in fact, an attacking shot if played well. It should be 'punched' in a flat arc into the rear corners of your opponent's court, travelling just above his outstretched racket to prevent interception and then 'dropping' quickly in the rear court region.

benefit to practise typical sequences in controlled situations by getting another player to feed you a set of shots that make up a typical sequence.

I must mention the importance of a strong overhead backhand for an attacking player. When possible, players generally attempt to hit round-the-head shots from their backhand rear corners. This is good because round-the-head shots can be particularly deceptive and powerful (in fact most top players are much more threatening when hitting round-the-head than when hitting from their forehand sides). However, an attacking player cannot afford to hang back in court in order to protect his weak backhand by ensuring he is always able to hit a round-the-head stroke. He needs to follow his attacking shots by powering towards the net in order to pressurize his opponents and snap up the weak returns. Sometimes he will be caught out and be forced to scurry backwards to retrieve a shuttle struck into his backhand rear corner. This is where a powerful backhand is important to enable the player to get out of an awkward situation by clearing the shuttle to his opponent's rear court.

A strong backhand can liberate a player, allowing him to risk pushing forward; a weak backhand leaves him always hesitant as he hangs back to protect this weakness. So, develop a good backhand; don't be frightened of it. Backhand overhead strokes require a good technique — *not* strength or power. Learn the technique and practise it every time you play. Although usually used defensively, a strong overhead backhand is an essential part of an attacking player's game.

In this short summary I have only been able to write about my broad strategy and, of course, I have ignored large areas of the game such as net play, defence, and service. Many top international players are highly successful without having very strong overhead attacking strokes. In this category I would place Morten Frost, Nick Yates, Xiong Guobao and Icuk Sugiarto. On the other hand, many of the world's most exciting players use the full spectrum of attacking moves.

Some players are particularly suited physically and temperamentally to a particular style but if you are playing men's singles for enjoyment and satisfaction I can assure you I find an attacking style the more rewarding.

Below: With his wrist cocked, Steve is able to block to the net or flick to the rear of the court.

Ladies' doubles *by Gillian Clark*

Over the last decade since the Chinese and Korean women appeared on the world badminton scene ladies' doubles has changed out of all recognition. The Asians have brought greater speed, strength and skill to an already physical and complex discipline. Long gone are the days when a good doubles partnership consisted of a strong rear court player and a sharp net player. Today's top pairs have to be masters of all the court. Whereas ladies' doubles used to be dominated by the forecourt player the game is nowadays controlled from the mid-court. Without strength and control in defence it is very hard to succeed in today's game. That is not to say ladies' doubles has become defensive; far from it, the attack has to be even more penetrating and accurate as it has become more difficult to find the openings and weaknesses in opponents' defences.

Most people agree that the speed and strength of ladies' doubles nowadays has increased considerably; not many recognise the higher skill level. In fact some would argue that virtually all the skill has been lost. I disagree strongly with these views. It is harder as a spectator to identify the vast skills of today's top players as opponents are so quick that shots which used to be outright winners are being met early and therefore giving no advantage. Therefore the skill needed to achieve that advantage has to be even higher.

Harmony

In doubles you are half a partnership.

Below: Gillian Clark covers a shot to the centre of the court while her partner Gillian Gowers looks on intently.

Two people playing together must first and foremost work for each other. Ladies' doubles is all about working in harmony with your partner developing the rally so that the opponents make a weak return for your partner to kill. A good doubles player has the ability to make her partner look good. This applies more than ever in today's game as women's defences have improved so much that it is almost impossible to make an outright winning smash from the back of the court.

The complete player

So what attributes does the individual player need to become a good ladies' doubles player? Technical skill, deception, tactical ability, fitness and a good mental approach. A weakness in any one of these areas will greatly affect the others and the player's whole game will fall apart. For instance, if a player is not fit enough as soon as she starts to feel tired her technical skill level will drop. If her mental approach is not correct her tactical ability will be affected. Therefore a high standard must be attained in all these areas.

Technical skill means having the ability to hit the shuttle to any place on your opponent's side of the court from anywhere on your side. This becomes more difficult when the game is played at a faster pace and so the individual player is put under more pressure. Not enough hitting skills are worked on and practised especially with youngsters. Too much emphasis is placed on quantity rather than the quality of stroke production. Without a good technique it is very difficult to become deceptive and you will lack a vital weapon.

One of the most important shots in doubles is the serve. It should not just be thought of as the shot that starts the rally but as the first positive move to make. Not only is a good serve hard to attack but the server should place the shuttle in such a position that she is able to anticipate the return. For instance if the receiver is inclined to hit a backhand push when you serve to the 'T' from the righthand court the

server should then be anticipating a return down the backhand side. Not enough people serve with the purpose of anticipating the return but to me these are probably the most important three shots of the rally.

I can't emphasise enough the importance of developing the vast variety of strokes and technical skills. Daily practices to strengthen the wrist are essential, for without a strong wrist it is very difficult to control the shuttle sufficiently, especially while defending. A good ladies' doubles player has the ability to turn defence into attack by driving the smash back or guiding it to the open space. Speed of reaction can also be affected by

Above: Gillian Clark is equally at home in all three departments of the game and is arguably the most talented lady player to emerge from British badminton within the last decade.

147

technique. If you have insufficient strength in your wrist the only way to gain enough power to get the shuttle to the back of the court is to use a full arm swing. The only problem with this is when you are put under pressure there is no time to use a swing, hence the importance of a strong wrist. Don't misunderstand the implications of 'strong'. In this context it means not so much physical strength but more the timing and technique. However, power and strength are a vital part of the ladies' doubles players' physical fitness programme. The fitness level required for ladies' doubles is just as high as that for singles but slightly different in that a doubles player requires more explosive power in her movement. Athletic leaps from side to side to cut out returns while in the forecourt, and jump smashes to gain the extra steepness and angle from the rearcourt are movements that must be worked on to produce the necessary power, speed and agility. Balance and poise are also essential in moving for without them recovery is slow which impedes the execution of the next shot. It is so important in ladies' doubles to hit and immediately move anticipating the return. There is no time to wait and see what the reply is going to be. Besides which every shot hit in ladies' doubles should be hit with a return in mind.

This brings me on to the tactics of ladies' doubles which are far too complex to go into in great detail. In very basic terms the idea is to manoeuvre and pressurize your opponents thus forcing them to make a weak return which can be killed. The best way to achieve this is by attacking. To stay on the attack, use the simple rule of only hitting down the middle of the court, which cuts down the angles of return, or hit to a position that ensures a weak reply that can be intercepted or killed. Tactical awareness can only be gained from experience but basically it is knowing the right moment to play the right

The most important factor in winning at ladies' doubles is

psychological attitude: the will to win, the determination, the agression and commitment; the guts and courage to take opportunities when they arise. Unlike singles, which is more about playing the percentage shots in a steady consistent game, ladies' doubles requires more risks to be taken. When you have that 50/50 opportunity at the net the good doubles player not only takes the chance of going for the kill but makes the winner. It is so important to remain mentally strong and confident. Even if your partner is going through a bad patch she can feed off your mental strength.

Ladies' doubles has so much to offer both participants and spectators and should not be overshadowed by the power of the men's doubles game. Ladies' doubles is a combination of speed, skill, determination and great tactical awareness. My enjoyment and enthusiasm for this discipline of the game is fired by all these complexities.

Opposite and above: In ladies' doubles, a high level of fitness is required to perform jump smashes and athletic leaps. A strong wrist is also essential when there is no time to use a swing.

Men's doubles *by Ray Stevens*

I was fortunate that my training for badminton came from a very solid foundation. Firstly, I was coached by an excellent coach, Frank Nevin, an art teacher at my senior school who had a real love for the game. He introduced a small group of young players to a top club, in Essex, England — Parkside badminton club. Their top team included two internationals, John and Bill Havers. I was soon playing for their teams and brothers John and Bill instil-

Below: Ray Stevens after delivering a short backhand service keeps his eyes on the shuttle to follow its flight.

led a standard that only the best was good enough, so much so that club night was often tougher than matches. I progressed quite rapidly through the county teams, playing many of my early first team matches with Bill Havers which gave a good mix of youth and experience. My big breakthrough came with selection for the international team at the age of 19. The competition was fierce, Derek Talbot and Elliot Stuart were our top pair, Dave Eddy and Eddie Sutton were a doubles pair that were regularly beating world-class opposition. Mike Tredgett and myself were in the same position. Soon people were recognizing that England had three world class pairs and there were only two places in the team. Competition helps to breed excellence.

The serve

The serve is an all important part of the game. The best servers I have seen in my career all had the same attributes. They developed their own style. Their action was consistent as was their serve. They blanked out the opposition concentrating only on their serve. They practised this department of their game regularly.

I have always taken the view that the less movement you have in your short doubles serve the better. It is more important that your swing is consistent. Try hooking your elbow into your lower ribs pointing your racket in a downward direction, with your wrist slightly cocked. Now let your natural body swing make the momentum necessary for the racket to strike the shuttle over the net. It is important that the shuttle travels flat over the net, not giving the receiver a chance to attack, even if this means it travels a foot further into the receiver's court.

Once you have found a comfortable service style that suits you, practise moving your service aim along the front service line practising your accuracy and finding your most consistent serve. This is the one to play at a pressure point when you have to get that serve into play.

If you find your opponents are pressurizing your short serve, this is a good time to bring in a flick serve. I suggested that the wrist be slightly cocked in the short service action, and for the flick all you do is uncock your wrist at the last moment. Getting the right height, trajectory and distance is all a matter of practice and concentration.

The backhand serve has distinct advantages over the forehand serve and is worth developing. A backhand serve is normally hit in a more forward position. The shuttle is that much closer to your opponent and this gives him less time to see the shuttle. This makes the backhand flick serve even more effective. An added advantage of the backhand serve being hit in front of you is that the white shuttle is difficult to see against white clothing.

The backhand serve can be hit with a forehand grip or a backhand grip. I favour the forehand grip and a short

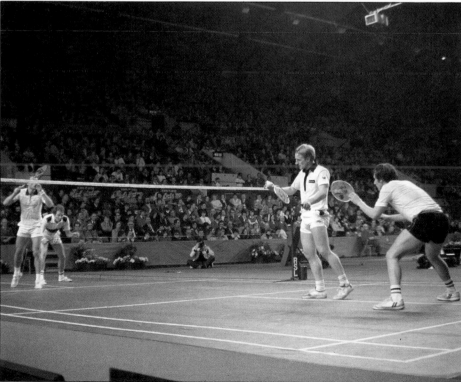

Above: Mike Tredgett preparing to serve with partner Ray Stevens close on his heels, fully concentrating with racket in front of his body in perfect readiness for the receiver's reply.

Left: As Mike serves, his partner Ray adopts a crouched stance with knees bent and weight on the balls of the feet, ready to move instantly in any direction.

Right: Ray Stevens, the former England number one singles player.

Opposite: Ray Stevens in action playing his favourite and extremely effective cross-court shot.

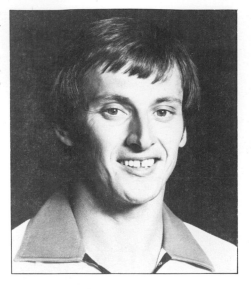

swing, aiming at the tape. I strike the shuttle firmly. A good consistent backhand serve is a very useful weapon in your armoury, and can be developed with practice.

Receipt of serve

Receipt of serve is about gaining the attack from the serving side, or ideally killing the shuttle where possible. To kill the shuttle means taking a forward position close to the front service line, threatening the server with an aggressive stance, ready to pounce on the serve and striking the shuttle downwards for an effective kill.

Effective places to gain attack or make kills

The receiver must be fit enough to cover the flick serve. To gain the attack you could use a stop shot to the net to force your opponent to lift. The main aim is to gain and maintain the attack.

There are two main formations in doubles: attack and defence. Attack has the greater percentage of success. In the attack formation one player is at the back playing attacking shots, his partner is in front of him around the front service line with his racket up in a ready position to cut out the returns or make a kill. I cannot emphasize enough the importance of learning the skill of holding your racket in a high position around the net level. A simple exercise is to get someone to drive a shuttle at net height, and the net player returns it using no stroke but the angle of his racket to stop the shuttle. This is a very effective way to maintain the attack and win points.

Defence

Defence formation is where players stand side by side, changing when the defender faces a cross-court smash, and he can afford to take a pace forward, as the smash has further to travel. The secret in defence is for both partners to play with rock steadiness to frustrate the opponents into turning the attack into defence. This counter-attack stems from taking the shuttle early, learning to drive, and playing into the openings between the two opponents a variety of strokes that allow you to lift, drive or block, but always looking for the opportunity to counter-attack.

The more you discuss with your partner how you are going to play your opponents the better. You might have picked up that one of your opponents only blocks straight to the net from a hard smash. That could be a match-winning piece of information if covered correctly.

The best pairs I have seen always work for each other, encourage each other, and think as one. Enjoy your game of badminton.

Mixed doubles *by Mike Tredgett, MBE*

Looking back in the history books to the game in years gone by, between the thirteenth and sixteenth centuries, the game used to be called shuttle-cock, featherball, and battledore. There are pictures showing Lady Henrietta Somerset playing with the Lord of the Manor, with solid bats, outdoors, which probably records the first mixed doubles badminton ever played.

Today's game brings together skills needed in both singles and doubles play, and combines all the ingredients, strength, deception, accuracy, grace, defence, and attack to name but a few. During my career, mixed doubles has always been the traditional club game and probably the most enjoyable.

Styles of play
When I started playing club badminton, I was told that the lady always takes every shot in the fore-court, and I was to take every shot in the rear and mid-court. As a starting principle, that's true. Most club, county and international pairs adopt this principle. Within the last five years the eastern countries such as China and Korea have been interested in mixed doubles and their style of play has brought a new dimension to the game. They have developed our style of play and trained the lady players to attack and defend to an equal standard as the male players, so it is like playing an even doubles team on the other side of the net.

Service
This is one of the most important strokes of the whole match. Mixed doubles is the only section of the game when a man and lady serve to each other. For the lady this can be very daunting. When a girl serves to her male opponent, she should think and concentrate on the net cord and practise short serving to the 'T' position, getting the shuttlecock as close to the net cord as possible. Generally, service is kept short to the man to make him play in the forecourt, ie out of position. To the lady a flick serve is often profitable, making the

Below: Mike Tredgett stretches 'round the head' to sustain the attack. His partner, Nora Perry, has her racket up ready to intercept any loose return.

partnership play out of position again and forcing the man to be aware of any return to the net. When the man is serving, it is best if the lady stands in the forecourt with racket up, but on the same half of the court as her partner. This allows the man to use the full half of the serving area for service.

Return of service

This is another important stroke. If an error is made here you have given your opponent a free point. The return tends to fall into three main types:

1 a winning shot from a poor serve,
2 a safe net shot building for a winning shot later in the rally,
3 a flat push from the net to the sideline at the rear or mid-court.

Your stance, ready to receive service, can often make the server's job easy or difficult. Best results are achieved if you are positioned towards the front service line on your toes, knees flexed ready to spring, with racket held above head height, keen and ready for the kill.

Playing cross-court

Generally there are only two positions in which it is safe to play the shuttle cross-court:

1 at the net, play the shuttle along the net at an acute angle. The lady will play this shot either to make a winning

shot or to get the shuttle lifted for her partner;
2 from the rear or mid-court, hit a full or steeper half smash to the feet of your opponents.

Never play a cross-court shot when lifting the shuttle from the rear or mid-court. Your lady opponent will be waiting with racket up to intercept it at the net. Likewise a flat shot from the net will be intercepted from the rear court.

Mixed doubles shots

All the shots played in singles and even doubles can be used and adapted for mixed doubles, but there are two or three that are unique to this department of the game.

Drive down the sidelines

The aim is to make the shuttlecock travel quickly and with as flat a trajectory as possible down your opponents' sidelines, deep into the rear court. Landing the shuttle in the back box is the ultimate aim, either as a winning shot or to produce a weak return allowing your partner the opportunity for a kill at the net.

Push to the mid-court

During a rally, when neither pair has an advantage, a push shot to your opponent's mid-court can often give you the advantage. This shot is played,

the lady of the partnership should be at the net with racket up ready for the kill.

Defence

You now have to prepare for your opponent to attack you, and this is where teamwork pays off. After playing a loose shot to the net, it is best if the lady stays at the net to try to return a drop shot played by your opponents. The return could be crossed at the net or could be a full underarm lift to be back of the court.

A loose shot played to your opponent's rear or mid-court requires different action. The lady must retreat from the net to adopt a side-by-side formation and try to return the shuttle to a position to allow defensive play to turn to attack again. There are four main defensive shots in mixed doubles:

1 a flat drive over the net,
2 an accurate return to the net,
3 a full lift to the base line, and
4 a flat push to the mid-court.

Deception

A disguised or deceptive shot in a rally can often give you the advantage. Skilled racket work can conceal from your opponents the true intention of your shot as late as possible. Two examples of these shots are:

1 a drop, clear and smash with the identical preparation and backswing. Only at the point of impact will the shot be determined.
2 a double action or 'faint'. This can be executed at the net or mid-court. The shuttle at the point of impact is played in a direction other than that suggested by your movements or racket face angle.

Accuracy

All shots played during a rally or match must be effective and accurate, using every bit of the court to expose your opponents. Unforced errors are not only frustrating, but lose matches. Your opponents won by you giving victory to them on a plate. Don't rush shots, think about the spot you want the shuttle to land in and play for it.

One of the best ways to become consistent and accurate is to practise

straight from your forecourt, mid- or rear court to your opponent's mid-court, the point just behind the lady player and in front of the man at the rear. This area of the court often brings the call of 'yours' and the result is confusion and a weak return.

Attack

This does not always mean trying to smash the shuttlecock through the floor, although when given the opportunity in the right position there is no more effective shot. Hitting the shuttlecock down at any pace, in any position on the court means you are continually on the attack. Winning shots can be:

1 a smash from the net,
2 a fast drop from rear to mid-court,
3 a slow drop.

When attacking, notice whether your opponent defends on the backhand or forehand side and play to the opposite. Attack on the weaker opponent, which is often but not always the lady. Use all the court when attacking and don't always hit or smash to the same spot. At all times shots over and over so that you can reproduce them, say 20 times out of 30, without error. Group several shots into a routine, so that the sequence can be reproduced time and time again in practice and during matches when the opportunities arises. These practices can be worked on during club nights.

Teamwork

The art of knowing where your partner is on court and which of you is going to move to take the next shot does not come easily to most combinations. It takes a lot of practice. One of the most important things to remember is that you don't have to make every winning shot yourself. During a rally try to set things up so that your partner can finish the rally. This rule applies to men and women equally.

Winning tactics

Probably the first time you will see your opponents in action will be during the knock-up before a match. Observe some important signs:

1 are they both right-handed players or is one left-handed;

2 is the backhand side weaker than the forehand, do they return more often on the backhand than the forehand;

3 do they serve backhand or forehand?

This vital information must be shared with your partner so a short tactical talk at the start of each match is essential. Try to get a good start in the first set, perhaps get to five points. Keep unforced errors to a minimum and force your opponents to make the mistakes. Be patient throughout the match and remember, if you are well up on your opponents' score, the game isn't won until you are shaking hands.

There will be periods throughout the match when one or both of you will not be playing well. Throwing your racket around the wall and sulking is not the best way to respond if your partner is having a troubled time. Encouragement is what is needed. Calm the situation down with, for example:

1 good quality serving;

2 getting into the attack;

3 cutting out unforced errors;

4 patience.

The place to have cross words, if any, with your partner is in the car park outside, not on court.

Attitude

Before you start a match, you should have a game plan in your mind and agree it with your partner. Have a positive attitude, be determined and have the will to win. More matches are won and lost in the mind before ever a shuttle is struck.

Left: Mike Tredgett and Nora Perry — one of the finest mixed doubles combinations the world has ever seen.

Index

Numerals in *italics* refer to illustrations

Acknowledgements
We would like to thank the following
photographers, agencies and
companies who very kindly allowed
us to reproduce their photographs in
this book:

Barry Bullough
Image Promotions
Northern Photographic Services
Peter Richardson
R.S.L. Ltd
Mike Torrington Sports Photography

Our thanks also go to the following
people:
Carole Brame for modelling for the
exercise artwork sequences
Helen Troke for modelling in many of
the photographic sequences
Photo Craft of Ipswich
Mike Torrington for taking the
photographic sequences